The Country That Lives Within Me

For Graeme W.

Thanks for your
support!

[signature]

NINA TRIFAN

The Country
That Lives
Within Me

A novel

UNIVERS

Cover image: Adobe Stock

Nina Trifan
The Country That Lives Within Me

EDITURA UNIVERS
www.edituraunivers.ro

ISBN 978-973-34-1686-9

for my son, Andrei
and for my husband, Florin

Attending to verbal constructs
makes care long-term,
not acute,

which is for the best
because, though flawed,
each one is salvageable

or replaceable
unlike my flesh.
Words can be compared

with moments,
houses, trees, wires,
wires, trees, houses.

All stand
on their marks.
Still,

there's a lot of overlap.
I move my eyes
to make time.

I take their measure
and create a duplicate.

The Job, Rae Armantrout

Lasciatemi cantare

I arrived in Toronto on February 26, 1990, the coldest day of the year. I was twenty-five years old. My parents disapproved. My friends shrugged off the news and moved on. My relatives and neighbours condemned me for being an ungrateful, insensitive daughter who neglected her duty to look after her parents. No one saw me off at the airport in Bucharest. No one waited for me when I landed at Toronto Pearson International Airport.

While I was waiting in line to go through immigration, I looked around at the sea of people, different ages and backgrounds, lured by a shared desire to give Canada a try.

"Miss, how much money did you bring with you?" the immigration officer asked me as he checked my documents.

"Ten thousand Canadian dollars."

"And where will you stay?"

"Yonge & Finch."

I was ready for tougher questioning and angry looks, but none of that happened. He stamped my landed immigrant papers in less than five minutes and off I went.

After I picked up my luggage I walked toward the exit.

"Miss, please come this way!" A man with a South Asian accent bundled up in a military-style red parka guided me toward the taxi line, his right hand respectfully touched his cap. All I could see from the earflaps of his ushanka hat was a pair of thick-rimmed glasses that made him look much older.

The cab driver put my two suitcases in the trunk, got in his seat and looked at me in the rear-view mirror when he asked for the address.

"Yonge & Finch, please," I said, putting on my seat belt, trying to sound like I knew this place – like I belonged.

A high school acquaintance had given me the contact details of someone she knew in North York. She had agreed to lease me her place. It was a condo building where a few owners rented out their places to newcomers like me. "To pay it forward," they had said. I didn't understand at the time. I wasn't accustomed to the generosity and kindness of people who were willing to give up their own comfort to bring relief to complete strangers only because they took the same path as them. The path of keeping only their memories, leaving their family and belongings behind to settle in a country that, one day, they hoped they could call home.

The drive on Highway 401, down to Yonge Street, was uneventful. A gloomy sky contained the whole city like a giant casting his shadow over us.

What if my family was right? What if my relatives, who saw no point in me leaving Romania, were wiser than I thought? What if this country had nothing to offer me, and the Promised Land was somewhere else?

I paid the driver who dropped me off in front of the building, and dialed 1104 on the intercom. A woman with a slight Spanish accent greeted me with exaggerated enthusiasm and told me to open the door when the buzzer went off. The lobby reminded me of the newly renovated hotels in downtown Bucharest. Icons of the post-communist décor wave, dominated by cheap leather, fake flower arrangements, abstract prints, and oversized floor-lamps whose ornate shades cast a dim light over low sofas generously covered in intricately woven silk cushions. A fusion style of bachelor minimalism, law office, and creative boutique in an affluent neighbourhood. A fortuitous convergence of Middle Eastern and Western culture.

With a short nod toward the concierge, I walked past his booth and took the elevator to the eleventh floor where I was going to meet my landlady, Mrs. Mendoza.

When I knocked on the door, I was expecting to see a middle-aged, overweight lady with a big 1980s hairstyle. Instead, in front of me was a beautiful woman with long dark hair who instantly reminded me of tango dancers entangled in a tight embrace, posing for the perfect picture.

"Good day, Ana. Nice to meet you," she said, shaking my hand with a strong grip.

"Oh, hi, I mean, good day, Mrs. Mendoza," I said.

I went in and waited by the door. Being in a place like Toronto where people spoke so many languages, some of them familiar to me, made me feel at ease.

"Call me Adriana, *por favor*," she said smiling.

'Sure, yes, ugh, thank you, *gracias*," I said.

Her husband Carlos stood up and came to greet me.

They showed me the condo and laid out the rental terms and conditions, asking me to sign the contract. They lowered the rent by two hundred dollars for the first three months.

"Until you get a job and settle in," Mrs. Mendoza said.

I paid cash.

They gave me the keys, left a piece of paper with their phone number on the kitchen counter, shook my hand again, and left, wishing me good luck.

I unpacked and went for a walk to explore the area. I felt lost among so many Asian, Middle Eastern, Italian, and fast-food restaurants. I didn't have time to observe the people walking past me. The fusion of aromas and odors that inundated the streets made me hungry. It was going to take me a couple of years to learn all those smells: curry, basil, freshly brewed Turkish coffee or roasted squash. Without paying too much attention, I entered the first restaurant that I found at Yonge and Empress Avenue. No sooner had I got in than a man greeted me in Italian.

"*Buongiorno, signorina. Come sta oggi?*" he said holding my hand as if we were old friends who agreed to have dinner together.

I pulled my hand and just stood there, trying to remember the few phrases that I had learned in university when I had developed a short passion for the Italian language.

In his late forties, with dark hair, and a charming smile, he was *l'italiano vero*. His red blazer paired with a white scarf would have made the 1980s famous Italian singer Toto Cutugno, who enchanted my adolescence, look like a cheap replica singing *L'italiano*, whose lyrics came to mind instantly: "*Lasciatemi cantare/con la chitarra in mano/ lasciatemi cantare/ sono L'italiano. Let me sing/Let me sing with my guitar in my hand/Let me sing/I am Italian.*" That guy was a true Italian.

I felt lost. I didn't want him to know I was new to the city, so I told him in rudimentary Italian that I was waiting for a friend, "*Sto aspettanda un'amica*." I felt like one of those women who kept wearing their wedding band even after a divorce only to keep people at bay. He smiled again and led me to a table by the window.

The square wooden table with two Tuscan vineyard placemats, chocolate brown rattan chairs, and a Mason jar candle on a tray of dried apricot and red sun roses looked like a retro postcard of the Umbrian countryside.

It was a small family restaurant with only a few tables. A young couple who spoke Italian glanced in my direction and giggled as they reached for each other's hands over the table. Two tables to their left, a woman who looked in her early fifties was checking her watch every five seconds.

Toto Cutugno in disguise brought me the menu and stood by the table waiting for me to order food and a drink. I asked for a glass of water and opened the leather-bound food bible. Twenty pages of pasta dishes, one of salads, and ten of drinks and desserts. The wine menu was separate. I didn't have the patience to read each description of multiple variations of pasta.

"*Signorina*, the special for today is our signature dish, chicken cacciatore, with a side dish of roasted potatoes and green beans. Do you want to try it? It's *delizioso*."

How could I go wrong with the special?

As I was enjoying an authentic espresso, a woman who seemed to be my age came to my table.

"May I?" she asked.

What was going on? Was that what people did in this city? Invite themselves to strangers' tables?

"I'm sorry. Do I know you?"

"I'm Katarina Lhotzky," she said waving at the waiter. "May I?" she repeated.

"Okay... Sure, please sit down," I said.

Pray & Dream

As an immigrant, I learned that people, like words, were broken, imprecise, unpredictable. I learned that, if you came from a dictatorship that stripped you of dignity through a culture of fear, Canada was a place to heal and grow.

After the Romanian Revolution that most viewed as a *coup d'état*, my home country opened its borders. Everyone was allowed to travel. After long years of dark communism, when the only plan was to hope it wouldn't get worse, people were still skeptical about their right to get a passport.

My parents felt like prisoners disbelieving their guards' promise to let them go.

"Ana, we're free, we're free," my dad said.

What an unimaginable adventure for people of my generation who had learned about Rome, Vatican City, Barcelona, New York, or Toronto only from geography books, banned radio stations, or stories of friends with relatives abroad.

On Christmas Day 1989, a firing squad executed dictator Nicolae Ceaușescu and his wife after a live show trial watched by millions of people. Not only in Romania, but all over the world. My parents cheered, our neighbours took up the street, the entire community celebrated. Self-proclaimed dissidents openly declared their opposition when they knew no persecution would occur.

Freedom was an added dimension to our lives, which most of us were afraid to explore. We were free to speak our minds, free to go wherever we wanted, free to buy anything. Store shelves were no longer empty, international aid was pouring in, news channels were commending the heroism of Romanians who reclaimed the roads of major cities and clenched hands in a collective prayer, thanking a God that seemed to have forgotten us. We were no longer victims of a totalitarian regime that had taken away our pride.

The doors to an expansive welcoming world opened and we could go anywhere we wanted. I didn't. Not right away.

After graduating from university in 1989, I landed an English teaching job at a middle school in the suburbs. Grade seven students were not exactly the type of crowd that I knew how to manage, nor were comrade teachers the kind of people I wanted to be friends with, but I learned my way through politics, acted as a substitute guidance counsellor on the side, while giving out awards to the brightest kids who read *The Catcher in the Rye* or *To Kill a Mockingbird*.

Although Russian and French were the two foreign languages of choice in most schools when I grew up, with the former being mandatory, English made its way into the curriculum as a second option starting in grade five. My eighth-grade English teacher who had personally met Constantin Noica, an iconoclastic Romanian philosopher harassed by the Communist regime, quoted his work between drills of irregular verbs and the sequence of tenses: "*Only in your own language you can remember things that you've never* learned." or "*Look at other skies, but dream only under the sky of your own world."*

I was too young to understand his audacity in citing the work of a political prisoner, but I loved his relentless curiosity, his persistence in challenging us with questions about how language shaped our thoughts and perceptions: "*Do words define who we are? How do they form our individual or collective identity? Do we trust emotions and mannerisms more than words when it comes to someone's character? If we were to compete with robots, which words would give us away? Which words would tell the enemy that we are human?*"

He never laughed at our puerile answers focused on phrases that labeled bodily functions, vocal tics, or stuffing words that we peppered our sentences with, *ugh, like, err, well.* A polyglot who believed in the supremacy of language over thought, he transformed his classes into linguistic manifestos – "*Le mot, l'image, le mythe, l'émotion, l'humour, le mystère, le rythme*[1]". He indiscriminately read to us while we hunched over our notebooks taking some random vocabulary quiz or testing our reading comprehension: Aimé Césaire, Stephen Rodefer, Carla Harryman, Susan Howe. His belief in poetry as knowledge and his obsession with the L=A=N=G=U=A=G=E poets influenced my decision to become a teacher.

In January 1990, three of my friends decided to leave Romania to work overseas at luxury resorts.

"Ana, we can go to New Zealand or Australia! We can go anywhere we want. You should come with us."

We had all graduated from the same program, with a double major in teaching and marketing communications.

---

[1] *Aimé Césaire – Poésie et connaissance (Poetry and Knowledge)*

One of my best friends took a job as a copywriter for a local creative agency specialized in political campaigns. Its founders, two computer science graduates with an uncontested love for pure mathematics, believed in the success of young politicians who advocated for social justice.

The bravest of my generation simply jumped on a train and got off at random stations along the route to Western Europe: Wien Westbahnhof, Munich, Brussels, Bergamo, Portbou. They found odd jobs on farms or in small factories, slept in shared houses, and every month they sent money home – the few schillings, Deutsche marks, francs, liras or pesetas they were able to save. The luckier ones were hired by rich Italian families as caregivers for their aging parents.

The allure of exotic places attracted mostly those who spoke a foreign language, those who chose to forfeit their future as teachers and engineers for a life that promised more than the constant struggle to make ends meet.

I stayed. I chose to teach. I worked in an educational environment plagued with favouritism and bribery, fueled by politics. Still. The school principal, Mr. Moraru, kept reprimanding me for disciplining students whose behaviour, in his view, was exemplary, especially if their parents were members of the Communist Party. Still.

"Ms. Sala, you can't do that. It will affect their overall grades, and that is unacceptable," Mr. Moraru lectured me every time I tried to exercise my authority.

I left my teaching job for a marketing position with a multinational company where, in a few months, I learned more than I did at university. The rise of brand management in an emerging economy offered opportunities and learning experiences better than any business school could get you. Some managers continued to pay homage to a lost world of status and privilege. Still.

The turmoil and uncertainty that followed the collapse of communism provided a fertile ground for other demagogues whose discourse, under the disguise of democratic values, pledged allegiance to the Romanian people. Everywhere I looked, I saw corruption and betrayal. Even my own language, once used to deconstruct poems and epistolary novels, started to fail me.

Luxury cruise ships were not an option for me, neither was working on a farm, so I decided to move to Canada.

Wenn schon, denn schon

After the initial shock of being befriended by a total stranger, I got to know Katarina over many walks in High Park, evening meals at the Mugshot Tavern on Bloor Street, and even more cups of latte and Kaffeekuchen at her house in Port Credit.

"Ana, do you know that Port Credit is called "the Village on the Lake?" she said.

Her Mississauga neighbourhood tucked away between the Queen Elizabeth Way (QEW) and the north shore of Lake Ontario got me hooked on nicknames of Canadian cities, terms of endearment coined by residents to express their love and affection for their communities. I started collecting them, like linguistic gems that satisfied my fascination with words: the Steelhead Capital of the World (Houston, BC), French Fry Capital of the World (Florenceville-Bristol, NB), the Diving Capital of Canada (Tobermory, ON).

When I met Katarina, I was struck by her Nordic features, and later by her perfectionism. We shared the same love for thoroughness and soon I found myself borrowing her German adages. "*Wenn schon, denn schon.*"

She dispelled many myths about typical German personality traits: she had a healthy sense of humour, she was diplomatic, and she was never punctual. She softened my Eastern European rough edges through her proclivity to make fun of all stereotypes, molding me into a naturalized Canadian proud of her new country, humbled by a new experience, and eager to show off her new identity.

"Ana, you're too negative. Embrace this change. Enjoy your new life," she said.

Her sunny personality attracted me right away. The daughter of immigrants who had moved to Canada in the late sixties, she told me she had always excelled in school and followed her father's advice to study psychology.

I admired her resilience, a toughness that she had learned how to hide, laughing away through life, hardening her soul to show others how to find kindness.

"Ana, I'm an ordinary woman living an ordinary life. It's only because of my Spartan upbringing and German background that I have ended up not disappointing my parents, really, by not marrying some weirdo or gallivanting off to India to pray alongside joyous devotees."

Her parents had come from Pentzberg, a little town located about fifty kilometers south of Munich, in Bavaria. After the local coal mine closed in 1966, Hanna and Jonas Lhotzky decided to follow a cousin in Canada, where they chose to live in Toronto.

It didn't take long for Katarina and me to become close friends. Her cynical nature, especially when it came to relationships, matched my Communist survivor syndrome: lack of trust, fear of persecution, and disdain for fake equality.

"Ana, shake off your mistrust in the authorities. This is not Romania. Cops are not corrupt. Or, at least, not all of them.

Unless you want to live the rest of your life wondering whether you belong here or not."

At first, she didn't believe all the stories I told her about what it had been like growing up under a Communist regime.

"You should write a book about that."

"Me? Writing a book? I don't think so."

* * *

I didn't know how to write, but I told her stories that I couldn't forget. And she listened. And she wanted to know more.

"Ana, tell me something about yourself," Katarina asked me every time we met.

It was like a game that we played over and over.

"I want to discover you piece by piece."

Like a puzzle whose parts you had to get one by one from a layered box with hidden compartments.

I told her about the five-mile walk to school that I did for six years until we moved to the city. Life on the outskirts was full of adventures. Fighting my way through waist-deep snow. Doing my homework at a toddler table that my parents had salvaged from a demolition site. Reading by the light of a kerosene lamp late into the night, sitting on the floor with my back toward the only gas heater in the house. Waiting in line for hours to get our rations of rice, bread, and cooking oil. Eating two pounds of bananas for Christmas at a single sitting because it was the only time of the year when tropical fruits were brought to the local store. Stealing the chocolate decorations off the Christmas tree. Craving Cuban lunch candies that were rarely brought in quantities large enough to last through major holidays.

"Ana, tell me something about yourself," Katarina asked me every time we met.

It was like a game that we played over and over.

"I want to discover you piece by piece."

The memories that I re-lived didn't follow any chronology or relevance. I told them as they came to me, letting her into my life, one story at a time.

"I grew up in a broken society governed by mistrust and disloyalty. Friends turning against friends, family members estranged over divided opinions about the Communist regime, antagonized neighbours turned into police informants spying on our conversations about Ceaușescu's dictatorship. A collective suspicion ruled my life, the suspicion that everyone was out to get me. Always cautious about how much I was willing to share, but still curious about how the isolationist mentality shaped our behaviour. I was predictable yet reserved. Skeptical. Apprehensive."

"Not the adventurous kind, I suppose. Running away or rebelling against your parents. Not someone whose disposition surprises you like dark roast coffee paired with salty peanuts instead of a rich decadent dessert. More like green tea and shortbread cookies, right? Yeah, I can see that in you," Katarina said as if she continued telling my own story.

Gele & buba

Nothing I had ever read about immigration, Canada, and settlement in a new country prepared me for what I encountered during my first weeks in Toronto. An avalanche of smells, faces, and colours. People with different accents talked to me in the grocery store, on the bus, in coffee shops. I frowned, nodded, used my hands more than I wished, and shook my head even more than I imagined. Coming from a country where English language teaching followed the proper British pronunciation gained by speaking with a pen between your teeth, I felt lost in a linguistic limbo.

But the most difficult part of my journey was finding a job. I wasn't born here. I wasn't a top graduate from a well-known university. But I had grit. I had work ethic. I knew how to chart my own path despite life's challenges. I had lived through the communist dictatorship that isolated entire generations from the outside world and crashed everyone's dreams in its engulfing power. I had to face my family's resentment when I announced my decision to leave my home country.

After a few failed attempts to get a marketing job through interviews where I had to answer some of the most unexpected questions and persuade my interviewers why they had to buy, for example, an exquisite pen for over one hundred dollars, Katarina introduced me to Obiaku who sent me to a marketing communications agency that he knew.

When I met him, he looked at me and declared, "You're a dark horse. A horse that enters the race with zero chances to win. A horse that everyone looks at and wonders who the heck placed a bet on that filly."

His detailed, pseudo-scientific story, flamboyantly delivered while holding my shoulders, lifted my spirits.

Obiaku proclaimed himself a horse watcher versus a people watcher.

"Ana, believe me, horses are more interesting creatures to observe than human beings."

I didn't know anything about horses, nor did I want to learn. But I knew Obiaku had met a lot of people like me in his assumed role of mentor to newcomers. He saw right through me, making it his mission to teach me how to navigate the system to feel included, integrated, immersed into Canadian culture. Then one day he invited me to an impromptu public speaking workshop at his house.

"You'll love it. Come. Bring your favourite food to share. Or your favourite wine. Or lemonade. Or whatever you want. Your favourite book. Just come."

I found a Romanian white wine at LCBO, Tamaioasa Romaneasca, that I hoped he would like. Peach, honey, and citrus. An aroma that reminded me of home.

Obiaku lived in a heritage house in the Annex on Spadina Road off Dupont Street. Although his family had done some renovations, they maintained its Edwardian style and personality, refinishing the tiles and the stained glass in the front windows.

I arrived late. The meeting was in full swing. I entered the living room where six people sat around an ottoman topped with books. An eclectic group of individuals of different ages and ethnicities gathered around an idea – how to maintain their identity while trying to fit in. Obiaku didn't bother to introduce me, so I sat next to a woman who looked majestic in a blue flower print head wrap and bright yellow top. After the meeting, I learned she had come from Nigeria and, because the gathering was a special occasion for her, she had decided to wear traditional clothing to make up for her western outfit, a pair of GAP jeans that she matched with the *gele*, a cloth wrapped around her head, and the *buba*, a loose fitting blouse with long sleeves that even men could wear. Her name was Ocheidike. She had come from the same region as Obiaku. A young woman with no family in Canada, she immediately became Obiaku's protégée. She followed him everywhere, watching him advise new Canadians on how to adjust. She took away the good from these interactions and left out the bad: the anger, the frustration, the disappointment that most of those families felt when they decided to give up their traditions to be able to move on.

Each guest had to tell a story about themselves. It could be a real story or a made-up one. A story that helped us learn something about each other.

I sat there watching them, envying the easiness of their words flowing toward me like a chatter of budgerigars, a mumbled conversation at times that made me wonder if it was a coincidence that we were all in the same room, sharing an experience that looked like initiation.

Their tapestry of stories spanning countries, ages, and cultures was a feast for my recently adjusted ear, struggling to understand so many different accents that Obiaku pointed out for me: Nigerian, Spanish, Punjabi, Cantonese, Mandarin, Polish, Russian. I learned recipes for Murg Makhani and other popular Indian dishes. I laughed at jokes about why Spanish speakers mispronounced "breakfast" or "special".

I listened to stories about genocide, revolutions, war, forced marriages, and female genital mutilation, stories of men and women who left their home countries behind and met in a random house in a Toronto neighbourhood to share their rites of passage and family dramas.

When it was my turn, I stuttered a few words of apology.

"Ahem, I don't have a story to share. Sorry, not tonight. I don't know what to say. Sorry, sorry."

"Come on, Ana. That's impossible. We all have stories to share. We're made of stories. What's yours? Why did you come to Canada? Tell us. You're among friends here," Obiaku said.

"Because it was the only way to feel completely free."

"That's it? That's not a story. That's a cliché. Tell us more," Ocheidike begged.

Everyone looked at me, expectantly.

"Well, I wanted to give Canada a try."

"Give Canada a try? That's not a story either, but we'll take it. Only if you promise that next time, you'll tell us a real story," said Obiaku.

"I love that. Give Canada a try," Ocheidike said leaning toward me, her words almost a whisper.

There was no next time at Obiaku's house. Not for me, at least. I didn't want to share my story with anyone.

I never saw Ocheidike again, but the image of her glowing skin in the light cast by a hand-dyed silk lampshade on the mantelpiece stayed with me for a long time. Obiaku told me that she found a job as an event planner for a non-profit organization that provided settlement services to new Canadians. That was a place where I hoped I would work one day. To pay it forward. Just like the people who rented their apartment to me. It was my turn to give back. One day. Maybe.

A few days after the storytelling night at his house, Obiaku helped me find my first job at a marketing communications agency where a friend of his worked.

"He owes me one," he said to me.

The agency was located at Yonge & Wellington, easy to get to by subway from where I lived. When I arrived, a panel of three people were sitting in a room not bigger than my new apartment. A round table with four chairs was the only furniture. I shook hands with them and tried to remember their names. Anjelica Sullivan, Jessica Gardner, and Keeran Owen.

They didn't hand me their business cards, but I could tell Keeran was in charge. He was sitting in the middle and the two girls looked at him every time they asked me a question. Anjelica almost rolled her eyes when I told her I had arrived in Canada a month before. Jessica smiled a lot and looked at me as if I were a stray dog that she was willing to adopt. Keeran was the only one who asked more technical questions. *Tell me about how you managed the brand architecture of your client portfolio. Give me an example of monolithic and freestanding brands. On average, what annual advertising and media budgets did you control?*

Every time he asked a question, he held eye contact as I spoke. He nodded and took notes throughout the interview that lasted almost one hour.

They offered me the job on the same day.

"Your boss is Brian Arlington, but he's on medical leave. You'll work with me for a while,' Keeran said.

The first two weeks went by fast. Then, one morning Keeran brought me coffee. Dark roast, black, tall size, but poured in a grande cup. And the morning after. And every morning after that.

Our first date was at a pizzeria close to the office after a late night, working on a project for a consumer packaged goods company that was planning a product launch in summer. On my way out, he stopped me and asked me if I was hungry. Until then, I hadn't socialized with anyone in the office.

"I'm starving," I said.

"Starving, eh? Then let's go grab a bite," he said, squeezing my shoulder.

The weather was warming up, so we sat on the patio. Wrapped in my scarf, I listened to his stories about Sudbury, his hometown, his university years as a graphic design student, his first girlfriend – a refugee from Somalia – about his aspiration to become a partner in the agency, not just a creative director.

"My parents were immigrants too. They came from Ireland. At first, they settled in Saint John, New Brunswick, Canada's Irish City. After a few years, they moved to Sudbury where they opened a used clothing store – or rather gently used, as they like to say – competing with Value Village and The Thrift Store. After five years, during which my dad completed his Chartered Professional Accountant designation, we moved to Toronto. When my dad retired from a financial services firm, we moved back to Sudbury."

He told me that their store, located at the corner of Elgin and Bradley Street in the historic downtown of Sudbury, continued to attract a steady flow of customers despite the recent condominium developments that brought along large retailers.

"My parents have made a small fortune; hard to guess if you think of the business itself," said Keeran.

He looked more Italian than Irish. His dark complexion and chestnut eyes gave him the appearance of a constant traveller whom you felt urged to ask what island he had just returned from. His smile invited me to open up and tell him about Romania and how I decided to emigrate.

"I really admire you, you know?" he said. "Coming here by yourself, without any family or friends to help you. That's a big decision. A great risk. That tells more about you than you can imagine. That shows fearlessness, and I like that in a woman," he said, touching my cheek with the back of his hand.

That was the moment when I knew. I knew he was the one.

As a newcomer, I still had that distrustful attitude, the conviction that nothing really was what it appeared to be. Uncrowned queen of *what if* scenarios, I proved everyone wrong when I fell for Keeran. My sudden interest in everything Canadian, from maple syrup to skating and the Canadian anthem surprised my friends back in Bucharest. Not only did I fall in love with everything Canadian, but I was dating a man who didn't speak my language and, despite his efforts to learn it, could not discern the subtle difference between the intrinsic goodness of "*mă*" and the jugular indolence of "*bă*".

Contrary to my expectations, Keeran liked my way of questioning everyone and everything. He found it attractive.

Every night after that, we went out. He had every date planned in detail. What time to leave the office, which movie to watch, what restaurant to eat at, what time to go to his place and cuddle up in front of the TV until late at night telling stories to each other until we fell asleep.

Everyone in the office was surprised when they found out about our relationship. When Keeran told them we were getting married, the reaction was pursed lips and awkward silence. It happened too quickly. Even I felt that way. He didn't seem to notice. He disregarded others' opinions or comments directed at him with a *je m'en fou* attitude that I envied.

"Why do you care about what they say about us? Let them talk. I don't care."

He didn't care? On the rare occasions when we socialized with co-workers, mostly client lunches and impromptu birthday celebrations, we acted as if we didn't know each other. Their caution around me conjured images of *les banlieues parisiennes*. Where did they think I had come from? From socially disenfranchised suburbs that produced second-class citizens?

We lived our own incognito story, a narrative woven around the simplicity of our life together: romantic dinners at family restaurants that served only one dish, frugal cheese and wine snacks in front of the TV, weekends away in small towns where we rummaged through used bookstores, eating fish and chips from greasy newspaper cones. I liked our game of surprises and innocent touches. I liked the way he kissed my temple claiming that spot as eternally his, how he reluctantly waved at me with his arm halfway up as if he didn't want to attract anyone's attention, how he held my elbow between his

31

thumb and index finger, firmly, but slightly aloof, a gesture of love, possession, and simple courtesy.

Katarina thought it was immature.

"I don't get it. It's absurd. Why can't he act like a man and be proud of you two being together?"

"That's not immature. Do you know what I think? You're jealous. Yeah, exactly. Because you wish you had what we have. Guess what? You're not my friend, because, if you were, you wouldn't judge me."

"Okay, listen, you're overreacting. I'll always be your friend, regardless of whether you like it or not. I'm not judging. I'm telling you that what he does is wrong because I care about you. Suit yourself. We'll see in a couple of years."

Katarina was a staunch skeptic with a penchant for demystifying my illusion of happily ever after. I liked to believe I was the product of my own decisions, that my life wasn't the random consequence of extraneous events controlled by my parents or someone else.

Our wedding wasn't grand in any way. Keeran's parents drove to Toronto on a Wednesday morning, met up with us at Nathan Philips Square, and came with us to the City Hall. They were the only guests at the brief ceremony and lunch at the Osgoode Hall restaurant where Keeran's dad used to be a regular when he worked in Toronto. He personally selected the mozzarella and roasted pepper focaccia toast, oysters, and scallion polenta fries for appetizers and strongly recommended the beef tenderloin served with wild mushrooms or the seared Digby scallops garnished with coriander and glazed almonds. We didn't even bother to check the wine menu, since he had already ordered it: a Grenache and Syrah blend with a powerful aroma and a spicy touch.

After trying to convince me that I had to wear a proper wedding dress which would have cost me fifteen hundred dollars, my mother-in-law gave up. I wore a green satin dress, just like the one my mom had on when they baptized me. I still remembered the picture hung up in my room: my parents facing each other in a loose embrace, hugging a white ruffled baby blanket wrapped around what I was told was me.

After we got married, Keeran's parents gave us money for a down payment on a semi-detached house at Yonge & Eglinton that we fell in love with. Built in the 1970s by an architect who lived there until he sold it to us, it stood out among the red brick houses with its raised stonework around grey window frames and a large burnt-red front door with an arched lintel. Keeran loved the red door because he believed it attracted positive energy, it showed a vibrant place which was perfect for a young couple like us. Keeran's mother, Colleen, a feng shui enthusiast, inculcated in him her obsession with how to organize furniture and place decorations in different corners of the house to bring more prosperity or health. She even did an energy map of the house and commanded us to put wood and water elements in the southeast area. We obliged. Keeran rarely disagreed with her, and I didn't care too much. Whatever made Keeran happy.

When we told her we were going to IKEA to pick up the furniture, she almost had a heart attack.

"Ana, honey, sweetie, my darling, come to your senses. Please listen to me. That's not for you and Keeran. IKEA is for the working class, for immigrants who come here dreaming about living in Toronto and have no idea they'll end up in poverty traps like those ghettos in France, what do they call them, I can't remember. Please be reasonable and make the right choice," she insisted.

An Ethan Allen devotee, Colleen desperately tried to convert me to her object of adoration. The only colour she ever favoured in her Ethan Allen sanctuary was coming from a lavender Cattleya orchid. Whenever she visited us, she brought one of their catalogues, trying to sell me on some furniture that was on sale.

"Honey, you do need a nice bedroom set. This IKEA furniture makes me sick."

Seeing someone who was selling used clothes for a living, but was carrying an Ethan Allen catalogue around, posing as this chic interior designer, was enough to humour me for months.

After several attempts, she gave up. But she never missed an occasion to remind me of my poor choices. Choices that made her uncomfortable when she described our house to her friends, even in front of us.

"Believe me. I told her, many times. She won't listen. She got this idea about functional furniture and modular pieces. That's too cluttered. Anyway, I'm wasting my time teaching someone like her the basics of interior design."

"Colleen, Ana's in the other room. She can hear you," one of her friends said.

"I don't care. She doesn't have the slightest idea about complementary and accent colours, which accessories should match which item, when to use floor versus table lamps, and how to control the light in a room," she said. And then, keeping her voice down, she added, "I don't even know what Keeran sees in her. Seriously."

When I told Keeran his mom had gone into a tirade about my lack of style, he dismissed the comment with a smile.

"You know she means no harm. Over the past couple of years, she's developed a passion for interior design and even volunteered to redecorate her friends' houses. She now thinks of herself as a famous designer, generous enough to share her brilliant insight into how to mix comfort with class, and divide the space based on purpose."

Even Keeran sounded like her.

Ferberize him

"Mom, don't worry! Everything will be fine. She'll adjust. She's smart. I know what you mean, but what can I do?" I heard Keeran on the phone as I came home from work one day.

When he heard the door, he hung up and came to say hi.

"Hey, whom were you talking to?"

"Hmm, my mom. She's bored. She calls me every day to ask about how your pregnancy is going, if we've picked a name for the baby. She wants to know if she can come over to paint the room. She picked up some *Good Night, Moon!* wallpaper to spruce up the nursery."

"Honey, I appreciate her efforts. But this is our baby. Can you, please, talk to her? I want us to do that. On our own."

"You know what she's like. She won't take 'no' for an answer. Would it kill you if she did it?"

"What exactly are you asking me? I told you what I want. But it looks like you don't care. Why do I feel we're always at her whim?"

"Okay, let's slow down. I'm sure it's the hormones talking. Why don't you lie down for half an hour? You must be tired. Let's talk about this later. Go, go," he said, shooing me from behind.

Maybe he was right, maybe I was overreacting. The pregnancy was going well, but I felt exhausted. The family doctor told me I was going to deliver a big baby, which scared me enough not to talk about it. Still, those nine months went like a breeze.

Eventually, Colleen took charge. She painted the nursery, planned a baby shower, and gave us lists of recommended names neatly printed on blue paper. Some of them were as eccentric as she: Gangero, Milou, Dormol, Pinter, Scavan. Others reminded me of the first puritans who arrived on the Mayflower: Dancell, Diewell, Helly, Ash. A few were what normal people would pick for their children without feeling embarrassed to call them on the playground: Elijah, Camden, Dominic, Norton. None of them were Romanian. When I brought that up, she dismissed me again. Swat, swat, swat, like a fly.

When my parents heard we were expecting, they congratulated us, but didn't show any interest in coming to Canada. To give us a hand or otherwise. Why would they?

My mom called to tell me I was out of my mind.

"Who is this man, anyway? You've been there since yesterday, and now you're having a baby? I can't believe it. I shouldn't have let you go there by yourself."

"Mom, I'm fine. Everything is going to be fine."

Just a few weeks left to go, and I still couldn't decide whether to take time off work or not. Hiring someone to look after the baby, as selfish as it sounded, was an option that I considered.

After Matthew was born, I was in bed for one week. Colleen was omnipresent – feeding the baby, cooking for Keeran, talking with neighbours, scheduling my appointments with the lactation consultant, cleaning, doing the laundry. Three times

37

a day, she would come into my room to bring me food and tell me to shake off the baby blues.

"Ana, when I was your age, no one talked about that. Yeah, I was sad, but I just cried a little, drank a little, and moved on. Who had time to babysit me? No one. My mother and my mother-in-law didn't give a damn about how I felt. It was my duty, my obligation even, to give birth and never complain. Like many generations before me. I don't know how your mom handled postpartum depression, but I would be really surprised if she did something different. I'm not saying you have that, or she had it, but especially in a country like Romania, right? I mean, what kind of support did women over there get? Anyway, eat your food and leave that bed. Your son needs you. Your husband needs you. And, besides, I can't live here forever. I have my own life."

Typical Colleen. She was giving with one hand and taking with the other. When I told Keeran, he assured me I was imagining her condescension. She was only trying to help. Swat, swat, swat. Just like his mom.

I took the year off. It was the best decision. What mother would say no to that? What mother would deprive her baby of that bond?

Life after the baby was like tumbling down off Death Road in Bolivia, and then getting lost in the Yungas forests. My days alternated between long periods of lethargy, pain, and low self-esteem linked into a perfect cycle that repeated ad nauseam. After the first month, Colleen stopped coming to our house. She called now and then to tell me about her social engagements, her most recent shopping trips to Niagara Falls outlet stores, or afternoon teas at the Windsor Arms Hotel.

"Ana, do you know that Katharine Hepburn and Elizabeth Taylor stayed at this hotel? Magnificent, isn't it?"

The few neurons that survived my pregnancy prevented me from grasping the magnificence of her experience.

"Oh, yeah? That's cool."

Keeran and I agreed to make Tuesdays and Saturdays our date evenings. Cuddle up after Matthew went to sleep, watch a movie, have a glass of wine. We did it only twice.

The first time he couldn't make it, he called from the office.

"Ana, I'm sorry, but I must work late tonight. I'll see you tomorrow when you wake up, okay? How's Matthew?"

"Yeah, sure. I'll be here, honey. Keeping a diaper change journal, feeding the baby, living the life."

He got busier and busier at work. Late nights and even a few days of travel per month became the routine, so it was mainly Matthew and me. During the day, my only interlude was a ride to the drive-through to pick up a tall Pike Place and a brownie or a slice of banana bread. Matthew fell asleep the moment I secured his seat, and then I drove around to enjoy my treat in complete silence. In the evening, we listened to Baby Einstein and read a stack of baby books supplied by Colleen: *Baby Faces*, *Where Is Baby's Belly Button?*, and an entire collection of *Pat the Bunny* or *Where's Spot?* Touch-and-feel books that made Matthew giggle.

Being a mother resembled none of the idealistic views I had before I got pregnant. Going for a family jog in the early morning, the baby resting peacefully in a big stroller, an angelic smile on his face. I got none of that. For the first couple of months, Matthew's colic kept me up at night, leaving me so exhausted that I resembled a madwoman. Each morning,

I looked so drained, with my hair matted with sweat and formula, and dark circles under my eyes that eventually became part of the new me.

"Ana, I don't know how your mom, or other women in Romania for that matter, raised their kids, but here, in North America, any mother who's laid her hands on a book or two in her life will let her baby cry. Don't go and pick him up when you hear a little whimper. I applied Dr. Ferber's method to Keeran. Take my word for it, it works."

By the time Matthew turned one, I was on a schedule that gave me the assurance I could handle anything. I didn't need Keeran or Colleen or someone else to tell me what to do, to give me advice on how to develop a bond with the baby, which words to teach him first, how long to ferberize him.

Dulce, galbenă gutuie

"A sweet, bright yellow quince, golden like my hair/Is ripening on the windowsill/Mom left it in my care. "Dulce, galbenă lumină/Cum și eu bălaie-eram/Mi-a pus mama o gutuie/Ce se coace-ncet la geam."

I loved singing this old Romanian song. It reminded me of childhood, my mom's pumpkin pie and baked quince that I was now preparing for the Thanksgiving dinner. Katarina joined us that night. It took me a while to convince Keeran. She had come to our house only once after I got married, when we threw a house-warming party.

"So, tell us about your crazy patients, Katarina!" Keeran said.

I stopped singing.

"What do you mean? What do you know about her patients?", I said. "Leave her alone!"

"Yeah, Keeran, what do you know about my patients?" Katarina said.

"Whoa, don't take it personally, honey! Are they or are they not crazy? They must be if they believe that coming to you and having you listen to their stories about their pathetic lives in badass neighbourhoods will solve their problems," he said.

"You know what? For a smart guy, you are quite ignorant. Why do I even bother?" Katarina said.

I always interfered in their ping-pong conversations.

"Cut it out, both of you," I said. "Can we enjoy this meal together?"

None of us did. That Thanksgiving was a complete fiasco. The overcooked turkey tasted like tree bark, and the rest of the meal was like salt on my wound. Even the baked quince.

When she left, I walked her to the car. Before she got in, she hugged me tight and kissed me on the forehead. We stayed like two lovers in a lost embrace, oblivious to the outside world. It may have been seconds, five minutes or half an hour. I couldn't tell. Once back inside, I pretended I was busy with the dishes.

Keeran had already put Matthew to bed and was drinking a glass of wine.

I couldn't even look at him. I hated his guts, I hated his arrogance, I hated myself for letting him treat my friend that way.

He came over and, facing me, burst into laughter.

"I can't believe you're getting upset again. What's the matter now? It seems like I can't get anything right with you. Tell me, woman, w-h-a-t i-s t-h-e p-r-o-b-l-e-m?" he said.

"Stop it! You'll wake up Matthew! You don't need to be so loud. Why can't you be nice to her? She's my only friend and you treat her like dirt. You keep picking on her. You force your opinions on her. You belittle her work. You always put her down. What's worse, you seem to enjoy doing that."

"I do. I'm surprised it took you so long to realize. I don't give a rat's ass about your friendship. Don't you find it ironic that only in highly developed countries, counselling and therapy have become the panacea to human suffering? No one knows how to struggle anymore. Look around you. All these

42

lackadaisical hipsters at our office who blame their failures on stress and childhood issues. They need to accept the inconvenient fact. Life. Is. Shit. Sometimes. And you must deal with it. Period. Lying on your therapist's couch and dissecting your inner life won't solve the problem. Getting a grip on reality will. What's more ironic is that your friend, who, I must admit, is a very smart woman, truly believes that her work helps these pathetic people."

"Well, that shows how insensitive and ignorant you are. She's a fine human being, devoted to her profession," I said.

"A fine human being? Listen to yourself! What does that even mean? Is that how you learned to speak English back in your home country? Like a nineteenth-century lawyer putting defendants on the witness stand to explain their motivations?" he said. Changing his voice to sound older, he continued, "Ladies and gentlemen, don't judge this young mother who gave birth to a baby addicted to opioids. She's not an irresponsible parent, but a fine human being; and this teenager who stole from his own grandmother is not a thief, but a fine human being, and this one over here, who bullied his children for many years, he's definitely a fine human being with some childhood issues."

"You're so mean, so mean."

I threw the tea towel on the stove and went upstairs into Matthew's room. I lay on the floor next to his crib and held his hand through the rail.

"Hi, my love," I whispered in the dark as the old Romanian folk song that I loved came rolling off my tongue.

"*Dulce, galbenă lumină,*
Cum şi eu bălaie-eram.

Mi-a pus mama o gutuie
Ce se coace-ncet la geam.
Aş muşca-o dar mă doare
Mă cuprinde-un fel de jind
Şi acum cînd trece anul
Parc-o simt îmbătrînind."

I left the room and kept singing to myself.

"A sweet, bright yellow quince, golden like my hair,
Is ripening on the windowsill – mom left it in my care.
I wish I could eat it or at least take a bite.
I wish I could touch it as it's shining in the moonlight.
But I waited too long; now, as winter's been forgotten,
It hurts to watch it getting rotten..."

* * *

When we started dating, I saw us as two islands joined together by some abnormal seismic wave, blending into each other until we became a country. The country of Keeran and Ana. Our secret place, with its own logic, rules, words, gestures, and memories. Not to be shared. Or forgotten. But one day, tiny, hairline cracks appeared in the ground. Little by little, crevices crisscrossed the land like a circuit board gone awry, with components soldered in backward. Our life together hadn't come with a troubleshooting manual or a logic analyzer. It was nicely packaged, but without instructions, just like a shiny device that seemed so intuitive, you didn't need a user's guide. Well, I didn't figure it out. Neither did he. We both failed.

Keeran was getting impatient with my grammar gaffes, my accent, my everything.

He said to me one day, "You should try those accent reduction classes. I've heard that there are a few firms in Toronto that offer this service to newcomers like you."

"Do I need one? Intelligibility has nothing to do with the accent. How can you be such a moron?"

"Moron, me? Because I'm being honest, and I tell you what you need to change?"

"Well, guess what? I don't need your honesty."

I didn't. I thought I had found someone who could accept me the way I was, someone who wasn't embarrassed by me, someone who could see beyond the clichés that others judged me by.

Days would pass by, and he would apologize.

"Ana, I'm sorry, I didn't mean to hurt you. Trust me."

I did. Trust. Him. And he did it. Again. And again. But I stayed.

We didn't have time for the vacations that we both wanted: trips to France or Italy, travel to Santa Fe for the Indian Art Festival, a 90-year-old native art market where we would have acquired little treasures for our so-called art collection.

Keeran convinced me to take some time off and go on a short vacation to Spain with my cousin Tudor and his wife. He offered to look after Matthew while I was gone. Without Colleen's help.

I took him up on his offer and went away for one week. Tudor had lived in Barcelona for several years before he moved back to Romania. I didn't know why he had chosen that city. He didn't, either. Overpopulated and polluted. The Catalan jingoism reminded him he wasn't a pure Catalan, therefore, he didn't belong. The trip was a fiasco. His wife Lea and I didn't get along well, and Tudor didn't make any attempts to reconcile our differences.

After a short tourist tribute to Gaudí, visiting Sagrada Familia, Casa Battló, Casa Milà and Parc Güell, we took the ferry to Mallorca where Tudor had rented a villa in Cala Llamp. I expected to see the ferry taken over by large Catalan families, dragging children, luggage, and pets with them. To my surprise, it was only tourists, most of them speaking languages that I didn't understand.

"How did you pick this place?" I asked him.

"Because Rafael Nadal was born right here, in Manacor."

My cousin, a tennis fanatic, had watched all of Nadal's games, cheering, swearing, yelling in front of the TV, and, like any respectable Romanian man who had a sports superhero, he felt compelled to see the birthplace of this young phenomenon.

I came back from that vacation even more confused than before. I couldn't blame Keeran entirely for what was happening between us. My life was falling apart. One day, I realized I couldn't fight anymore. I couldn't go on living in a shell, lying to myself that nothing had changed.

I had to accept that the romance faded away. That nothing was the same. Or maybe we still had a chance.

"Ana, let's go away for the long weekend in August," he said. "My mom can look after Matthew."

"Let's."

At the beginning, we went on trips to inconspicuous places in Ontario and Quebec like Dorset, Maynooth, Sorel or La Tuque. We didn't mind driving. Keeran had a penchant for bed and breakfast places that creeped me out, owned by retired professors who made it their life mission to quiz their guests on social injustice issues plaguing Latin American countries, nationalistic views and anti-immigration movements sweeping through the European Union, expense report scandals tainting Canadian senators' reputation, or the viability of ethnic enclaves in multicultural societies that ultimately discouraged various groups from cultural assimilation.

If it hadn't been one of these topics, it would have been a debate over the right to buy versus adopt a dog.

Keeran enjoyed talking about that kind of stuff.

"Ana, you're so uptight about this matter. How can you not find it at least remotely intellectually challenging?"

"Let me tell you what I find intellectually challenging. The fact that you fall into this trap every time. The trap of listening to bored retirees pontificating about social science and international affairs like self-proclaimed gods in front of impromptu audiences, whose only connection with the outside world, besides CBC Radio, are the newspapers left behind by their guests when they check out."

"Oh, take it easy, you always take everything personally."

"Do I? I find them so fake, so condescending."

"Is that so? Why don't you ever participate in these conversations? You just sit there, judging them. It's easier than having an opinion, isn't it?"

"Easier than having an opinion? Listen to yourself. You're the one who's judging. You know what? Never mind."

It felt like we couldn't get anything right anymore. Those excursions accentuated our divergences in ways that Keeran found "irreconcilable."

"Ana, there are irreconcilable differences between us," he said when we got home from one of our trips.

He went to sleep in the guest bedroom, and I watched a movie with Matthew.

"Mommy, is the barracuda going to eat the dolphin?" he asked.

"No, honey, it's not," I said hugging him as he curled up on my lap.

"Why? Because they wanted it to be a good story?" he said.

"Yes, I guess you can put it that way," I said.

A happy ending story. That was what I had dreamed of when I married Keeran. I was attracted to what he meant to me as a newcomer. A Canadian man who chose me. Who didn't care about what his parents thought of me. Who didn't give a shit about what his friends thought. Or anyone else. Except his mom. That was only at the beginning.

I had the photo album that Colleen gave us at our wedding. I chuckled as I browsed through hundreds of pictures of Keeran growing up and saw the same décor popping up in his family snapshots. The living room washed out in the afternoon sunlight, with its Ethan Allen Romance signature line filling up the small space. The sandblasted coffee table ostentatiously topped with architecture and home décor magazines placed in front of a white Bennett sofa with walnut finished armrests, matching chairs with tapered legs, and side tables accented with crystal table lamps that looked like trophies.

I sank deeper into the loveseat, holding Matthew who was still watching the movie, unaware that my thoughts took me back to a time when I thought my life was picture-perfect.

"Mommy, I'm tired. Can we go to bed now?"

The movie was almost over anyway, so I put the photo album away and took him upstairs to give him a bath.

After that, Matthew came into our room and sat on my lap.

"Mommy, why did the dolphin leave his pod?" he asked, turning his head and resting it on my chest.

"Because he wanted to follow his dream," I said.

"What was his dream, Mommy?"

"To explore the world," I said.

"Mommy, did you follow your dream?" he said.

I stroked his hair while pulling him close.

"Mommy, did you follow your dream?" he asked again.

"Yes, yes, I think I did."

"What was your dream?"

"To have you."

"Did you have to leave your pod, too?"

"Yes, I did. We can talk about this tomorrow. It's late. You should go to bed."

For many nights after that, Keeran slept in the guest bedroom that became his domain.

We acted like two roommates who shared a kitchen and a little boy. Days came and went, our lives stuck in a state of inertia. Two strangers running on autopilot, faking smiles at each other, waiting for the other one to give up first.

One night, after Matthew went to sleep, Keeran came into my room.

"Ana, we need to talk."

He sat on my bed, our bed, crossed his arms, and looked at me.

"We're both so unhappy that we'll do ourselves a favour by going our separate ways. I thought this would work, us would work, but I was wrong. You don't need to say anything. Don't even try to disagree with me. I know you'll lie. Admit it. You're

49

miserable, too. Ana, I'll give you an A+ for your effort. You've tried very hard, but let's face it. We are not meant for each other."

He gave me an A+? What the fuck was he talking about? What was that? A high school drama? How about I gave him an F for faking it?

"I can't believe we're breaking up. After all the family shit that I've put up with. Your mom who judges me every second of my life, splitting hairs over the colour of my shoes or my distaste of expensive décor? And your dad? Don't tell me he likes me. I know how controlling he is. Even at our wedding. You didn't get to pick anything – from restaurant location to food and wine. I bet their greatest disappointment is that they didn't get to pick a wife for you."

"Now you're overreacting. That's your style."

"My style? What do you know about my style? What do you really know about me?"

Then I told him how much I loved him, and how I wanted him to stay. He looked at me as if I didn't even exist. The child that we had together wasn't the fruit of our love, but of pain, misery, and deceit. I didn't even love him. Or maybe I did. Yes, I did love him. I wanted him to say something that would dissipate the pain, the numbness, something that would wake me up from what felt like an endless slumber. I kept looking at him. Words refused to come out. I didn't want him to leave. I wanted our son to grow up in a family, a whole one, where mom and dad were happy, and angry, and sad, and demanding, and welcoming, and forgiving. A family where parents were always there. I didn't want my son to grow up rootless like me, thrown into the world like a yarn ball unravelling in its path. I bit my fingernails, cracked my knuckles, smoothed out the imaginary wrinkles on my black Calvin Klein dress. Words refused to come out.

"I'm sorry. I didn't want it to end this way. I have someone else. I'll move out next week. And I found another job. I'm leaving the agency."

"You did? No, I'm moving out. You stay."

He had someone else. Who was it? No warning. For him, it was business as usual. He was moving out. I wasn't going to give him the satisfaction. I was moving out.

"Ana, don't even say we should patch things up!"

Patch things up. Patch things up! Who was this man? What the fuck was he talking about? Patch our life like a piece of gobelin needlepoint you could stitch over and over again? Or maybe one of those vintage slide projectors you could buy on eBay, play with them for a while, change up the slides, project a silent movie on a blank wall for one night, then toss it in the garbage.

I told him I needed him. Again. Out of nowhere, I started telling him about my dad when I was little. How I used to hide behind my bed when I heard his footsteps at the door. I knew by how he walked if it was going to be a good night or not. Clutching a cloth doll in my hands, I closed my eyes and prayed to a God I didn't understand, please, please, make him turn around and leave me alone. As I grew up, I relived this moment so many times that it felt not like a memory, but a recurring dream about monsters hidden in the walls, coming alive at night when everyone was fast asleep, when no one was watching.

I must have looked like a lunatic blabbering away about a scared little girl hidden in a dark room. I even told Keeran how I wanted Matthew to be brave, how I didn't want my son, our son to ever be afraid or have to hide. I begged him to stay. Promised him I would change, although I wasn't sure I knew what I had to change or how I was supposed to behave, how I could be someone else. His frozen eyes gave him an android look that sent an electric shock down my spine.

That was the moment I knew I had been wrong about him. He wasn't the one.

Soon after that, he moved out. And in with his new girlfriend, Devin, a young woman from the office. Devin. Androgynous names always made me uncomfortable. Why did parents confuse their children with names that didn't denote their gender in any way?

They both left the agency, so I was happy I didn't have to run into them when I went to work. They bought a condo on Wellesley and Bay Street, close to the subway station. Their new office was downtown, so it was a convenient location.

It happened so quickly. I didn't even have time to process the entire episode. It was over. That, I knew for sure.

Wahre Liebe stirbt nie

How was I going to make a new life for me and Matthew?

"Honey, you have to RE-BUILD your life," my mom said when she called me from Romania.

I never quite understood how you could re-build a life. Was your life like a house that had been demolished, and you decided to erect a new building on the same piece of land? You hired a new architect, a different builder, trying to give it the same character, similar landscaping, a consistent colour scheme, but you knew it wasn't the same house. It was like a broken vase whose shattered pieces you could glue together to hide your clumsiness, but you knew the pot would never be the same, because deep down under what seemed like a perfect restoration there lay the proof of its damage.

My friends rallied to support me through the divorce. Katarina was the one who put me in touch with a real estate agent who found me a home in Mississauga. It was on a cul-de-sac lined with chestnut trees in an old Italian neighbourhood where even the street names had the resonance of Romance languages – Corso Umberto, Alessandro Volta, Santa Marta Avenue, Sermonetta.

From the kitchen that was facing the street, I could hear flip flops echoing off the sidewalks, and children screeching in the playground.

Roller blades, strollers, barking dogs, ice cream trucks, burnt hot dogs, live music, screaming going-down-the-slide kids, angry parents yelling in thick Italian accents or mangled English.

I could taste the smoke on the hot dog handed out by Milan, the old Serbian guy, to the loyal customers waiting patiently in line. Enough smoke to make you thirsty. Not too much to ruin the food, but enough to remind you of Eastern European meat shops sprawling the outskirts of Toronto in response to growing communities of Polish, Czech, Ukrainian, Romanian, and Hungarian immigrants.

If I closed my eyes, I could imagine what the playground looked like. Bolder kids desperately hanging down the monkey bars, screaming at their parents to catch them. Five-year-old girls in pink capris and matching studded princess shirts waving their hands in the air to show off their nail polish. Toddlers making their way up the stairs toward the lower slide. Babies crawling in the sand, sucking the grit off their thumbs as dignified grownups lectured them from the side. Bichons with baby-doll faces licking off the swings. A few teenagers playing ball on the grass soccer field stretching close to fenced million-dollar houses on Mississauga Road.

Evenings were the worst. The cold bed sheets, the empty room, the complete silence after Matthew fell asleep. I switched to old lady thermal pajamas whose sole purpose was to keep me warm. Tucked in under the comforter, I cried myself to sleep, the door closed so Matthew couldn't hear me.

It wasn't only the evenings. It was the mornings when I woke up alone, with no one on the other side of the bed, no man against whose warm sleepy body I could push my cold feet. It was the blank moments during the day when something angered me at work, and I had no one to call and vent. It was the dead time spent in the grocery checkout line without a conversation buddy. It was at bath time when Matthew asked about his dad as if he hadn't realized that he had been gone.

Every morning, I faked a cheery voice that almost made me believe everything would turn out okay.

"Mom, what's for breakfast?" Matthew would yell from his room seconds after he opened his eyes.

The Saturday pancake and Sunday scrambled eggs tradition was the only routine that reminded both of us of the mornings when our family of three sat on the kitchen bench, making plans for the weekend ahead. "Dad, can we go see the planes again, please?" After his first trip to the Canadian Warplane Heritage Museum, Matthew developed a love for everything related to flying. "Of course we can. Let's see who's going to be ready first," Keeran would challenge him.

"Mom, helloo, what's for breakfast? Did you hear me?" Matthew would ask again.

Wait. What day was it? Yesterday was… what was it? Monday or Tuesday? It was a weekday for sure; it didn't matter.

"Where is he, Mommy? Where did he go? When is he coming home? He doesn't love me anymore," he said.

"He's not coming back, honey. I've told you. He still loves you, but he wants to live with someone else."

"Why does he want to live with someone else? Because I'm a bad kid?"

"No, you're not a bad kid. Don't you ever say that."

Sleep became a panacea for all my anxieties. It sounded like, "I don't want to talk about it. It's time to go to bed." or "It doesn't matter. It's time to go to bed." or "Let's talk about it tomorrow.

It's time to go to bed." It was a conversation ending that gave me hope. Hope that, if I were going to sleep on it, I would have an epiphany. I would wake up the following morning enlightened on how to handle life or how to escape to a place where no one knew me.

I heard many stories of people who suffered from dissociative fugue. A temporary amnesia that forced them into assuming a new identity after they lost their memory. How tempting was the idea of fleeing your own life, escaping the present and replacing it with a more meaningful one? A liberating feeling that broke away with a traumatic or just heartbreaking past. I imagined I would take the subway to Union Station and then get on a VIA Rail train to Western Canada. Ponder all the stops on the way until I picked one based on the scenery – prairies or mountains? I would choose the Rockies for their promise of majestic serenity, leave everything behind, start anew. A new me in a new place that didn't have the burden of my past. I would get off the train at a random station like Hope or Vanderhoof, find a B&B, and then get a job at the local library. Maybe fugue didn't even exist as a condition or disorder; maybe it was made up by people like me who lacked the courage to face their inner demons.

* * *

"Mom, you are my little mango."
"And you are my little peach."
"You are my little pineapple."
"And you are my little pumpkin."
"Mommy, are pumpkins fat?"
"Some are big. Why?"

56

"I'm not fat."

"No, you aren't, honey."

"I love you, Mommy."

"I love you, too, Matthew. Now go to bed, it's late." I tucked him in and sat on the bed by his side.

"Can we read one more book?" he asked. "Read '*It's time to sleep, my love!*'"

I grabbed the book from the floor and looked at Katarina who was standing in the doorway.

I loved that book. A comforting, poetic lullaby that helped me calm down as Matthew was falling asleep.

> *"It's time to sleep, it's time to sleep,*
> *The fishes croon in waters deep,*
> *The songbirds sing in trees above,*
> *It's time to sleep, my love, my love."*

That was our bedtime ritual since Matthew turned two. Curled up in bed, his head resting on my chest, we would read a book, and make up our own stories.

He loved the cloud-shaped night light that Keeran's mother had given him on his first birthday.

After he fell asleep, I took the light out and went into the living room. Why was he so attached to a present from my in-laws?

"Katarina, I feel lonely without Keeran."

She shook her head and pretended she had to find some tiny item hidden in her oversized purple Michael Kors tote which I used to call her 'mini convenience store'.

She smiled, touching her blonde hair with her left hand. I found this gesture of hers fascinating, extremely sexy.

"*Wahre Liebe stirbt nie. Wahre Liebe stirbt nie*," she said.

"What did you say? That true love never dies?"

"Wow, not only did you hear what I said, but you also know what it means. You see what happens when you spend too much time with a German?", she gave me a quizzical look that always made me laugh.

What did she know about love? She wasn't married and never told me about any of her intimate relationships, if she ever had any.

Her mix of English and German phrases made her irresistible. I kissed her on the forehead and went into the kitchen to get my wine.

Katarina was always there for me. I called her in the middle of the night. I called her during her therapy sessions with clients who were more messed-up than I was. I called her when she was on vacation with an old friend. I called her regardless of the time of day or night, without caring whether she was busy, whether she had a life. And she never said "No."

"Hey, guess what?" she said, still busying herself with her bag. "I've brought my pajamas for a sleepover. Isn't that fun?"

I guess. I had nothing better to do than stay up late to chitchat and watch movies.

The next morning, she woke up before us and made blueberry pancakes which we ate with maple syrup and acacia honey.

"Where did you get the acacia honey from?" I asked her.

"From a Romanian client. He went back to visit his family and brought me a jar." She was beaming.

"This is my favourite honey," I said.

"I know." She patted me on the back and burst into laughter.

We ate our pancakes in silence, enjoying the freshly ground coffee brewed in my old French press. Another perfect morning.

Matthew ate his breakfast in silence and then went to watch Thomas the Train on my laptop that I kept on a side table low enough for him to reach.

"What's the retirement age in Canada?"

"What's come over you? You're only thirty-two. What now? Are you filthy rich and you don't need a job anymore? Or are we breaking up?"

I laughed, trying to imagine Katarina in a stable relationship, disheartened by the many chores of a big household, kids constantly running around, a dog that had to be walked three times a day, a mother-in-law bickering about the bad fate that consumed her progeny, a gossipmonger living next door relentlessly starting rumours about all the neighbours. It was a picture that didn't fit her.

"Ana, I'm not made for marriage or any other form of long-term commitment. You know that," she said as if she had read my mind. "Relationships are like wars. More difficult to end than to keep them going."

I knew she wasn't, but it gave me pleasure visualizing family scenes like big oil paintings with an aperture in the middle where, in the blink of an eye, you could step in and slide into a different world. Instead of a fantasy land populated by anthropomorphic creatures, you would find a world of secrets, shame, guilt and remorse; a hidden world inhabited by people who never told the truth. A world of contriteness, of frugal gestures, and lost love.

"So, what's the plan for today?" Katarina asked. "What do you have in mind? Where do you want to go? What do you want to do? Tell me. Tell me."

I didn't have any plans. Matthew was going to spend the weekend with his dad. My life followed a sinuous path of acceptance and deception, of unplanned events that didn't have the burden of commitments.

"I don't have any plans, Katarina. You know very well that I stopped making weekend plans."

* * *

On the weekends that Matthew spent with Keeran, and Katarina was too tired to come over, I stayed home and watched videos of Matthew. There was one Saturday that remained in my memory. It was late October. The smell of burnt leaves and pumpkin pie made me crave family reunions. I missed the togetherness, the popcorn and movie nights, the reading clubs when the three of us would cuddle up in our king size bed, blanket pulled up to our chins, Keeran or I were reading aloud *Franklin the Turtle* and *Curious George*.

The first video was one of Matthew at one and a half years old, standing by the window, talking to squirrels. His plum-shaped cheeks and chubby hands took up the whole screen in a bad close-up as he reached out toward the open window to catch a chipmunk. He was wearing navy blue twill pants and a red long sleeve shirt whose front was embroidered with BSE, a personalized present from Keeran: Best Son Ever.

"Squillel. Squillels eat seeds," he said in a thin reedy voice.

His movement looked like a slow dance on screen, a swirl of blended colours, shifting from blue to red in a continuous loop. I closed my eyes. All I could hear was his muffled voice, and I imagined him running from the window to his IKEA table in the corner, banging some makeshift drumstick – a wooden spoon or a Tupperware lid – on the chair, pretending he was fixing it, or touching his Leapfrog fridge phonics magnets, swinging back and forth as he sounded out the letters.

I opened my eyes at the end of the video. I took another disc and watched Matthew in a different setting. A tiny man wobbling among Japanese cherry trees, mauve rhododendrons, and blooming azaleas in the Rhododendron Garden in Mississauga in late May. The sunlight reflected through tree branches looked like frayed lace on a dip-dyed shirt.

"Mommy, come, come," he said. His voice, like a chirping sound, blended in with the eerie symphony performed by a chorus of birds flapping their wings. I watched myself joining Matthew in his toddler trot, running in a circle, laughing, throwing ourselves on the ground, holding hands, making 'grass angels'. The last image was of Matthew climbing on me, his little feet pushing down on my arms and my chest, making me look like Gulliver on the island of Lilliput.

Oxygène & Équinoxe

After the divorce, I filtered out all the noise in my life. Self-entitled friends who gave me advice on what to do to get over my ex, well-meant neighbours who wanted to hook me up with their second uncle's cousin's son. Tell them to shove it? The advice, that was. Or smile politely and decline their invitation for Martinis and vegan burgers due to a prior commitment to binge eat Nürnberger Rostbratwurst garnished with sauerkraut, potatoes, and horseradish?

The house that Matthew and I moved into looked more like a vacation rental than a permanent place, despite my attempt to make it look like home: I cooked every day, I hung up clothes to dry in the laundry room, I let Matthew clutter the living room with his toys and pop-up picture books about faraway perfect families on a faraway perfect land. We continued to create memories that no longer included a dad. Or rather they included a weekend dad or an absent dad. It dawned on me that the weekend parenting books I had often seen in the self-help section at Chapters Indigo were meant for people like Keeran: poster dads whose preoccupation with their self-worth always took priority over changing diapers or picking up their kid from daycare.

"Mom, can we get a puppy, please, pretty please?" Matthew pleaded with me every time we watched *Lady and the Tramp*.

The idea seemed ludicrous. An untrained puppy pooping and peeing all over the house? No way.

"Honey, I can't handle a dog now. I'm still trying to figure out how to handle life."

I swore that if I had ever decided to get a puppy, it would have had Matthew's eyes: begging, bewildered, curious.

Keeran called every Thursday night, the day when his girlfriend Devin went to yoga classes. Matthew liked to put him on speaker. One time when he called, his voice was interrupted by clattering pots, the humming of a range vent hood, food-mixing spoons.

"Dad, I'm colouring Thomas the Train. What are you doing?" Matthew asked.

"I'm cooking, bud."

"I didn't know you could cook."

Neither did I. I could hear Jean-Michel Jarre playing in the background, one of the musicians that had captivated my teenage years when I used to fall asleep with his Oxygène and Équinoxe cassette running on a Sanyo player next to my bed.

"Dad, am I coming to your house this weekend?" Matthew asked.

"No, bud. Sorry, I can't, I have other plans. Can you, please, put your mom on the phone?"

He had plans. Long weekends were not for kids. They were going away. Again.

I took the phone from Matthew and listened to Keeran's excuses.

"Ana, sorry to do this to you again. But Devin and I are going away. Can I take Matthew next weekend? I promise I'll come and pick him up early."

"Yeah, no problem," I said, hanging up.

For the first six months after we broke up, I called Katarina every day. A marriage counsellor having her own private practice, Katarina had serious trouble believing in long-term commitments. Although she had counselled couples for over a decade, she never got married.

"Ana, I've seen way too much sadness, too many fights, too much hurting. I couldn't go through this. Most couples that come to see me don't even realize their unhappiness comes from the fact that they expect to make each other happy. When I try and tell them that they have to make themselves happy, and not expect their spouse to do that for them, they look me blank in the eyes and I can see their disagreement. I tell most of my patients to write everything down. Believe me, it helps. You should try it."

* * *

Words always saved me. Words that came to me like a dovecote lifting me up, letting me fly on their backs, taking me to places I had only dreamt of. Words healed, but also hurt, like a cauldron of crows knocking me off my feet.

Katarina said I should keep a diary.

"Write every day. Write when you feel lonely, or sad, or happy, or whenever you want. Write about anything. Your despair. Your solitude. Your joy. Your everything. Don't underestimate the power of words," she said.

For many months, I woke up half an hour before Matthew and wrote in this orange leather-bound journal that Keeran gave me after he had hired me.

Two hundred pages, fifty of which I covered in doodles during meetings; countless hours of meaningless quibbles over which tagline to choose for a particular campaign or which brand name better represented a new cereal mix. At first, I didn't know what to write about. To me, writing was a profession for the chosen few, an activity reserved for bestselling authors, and I found journals frivolous.

But I trusted Katarina, so I kept going. There were days when the only words I could write were what was left over after I had lost everything. Love. Hurts. Too. Much. And. Life. Sucks. On the better days, I opened the windows and let the morning air bring in the sounds and smells of the city. It was easier to write about squirrels eating acorns or chestnuts, about blue jays flying through leafless branches screeching in pain, or dogs barking in the distance.

Other times, I wrote about how Keeran and I had met, how we started dating, how we made each day count, every weekend.

* * *

"To bounce back after a breakup, you need at least one month for each year spent together with Keeran," Katarina said.

That made it four months for me, but it wasn't enough. The unbearable pain, the emptiness that reminded me I had failed was too much. I had failed at relationships. Was I failing at parenting too? The only way to redeem myself was to raise Matthew into a strong, confident young man unafraid to talk about his feelings, willing to take risks.

Loneliness was mine to bear. Even the simple gesture of pouring coffee in the morning made my body ache. My hands clenched on the French press felt like a foreign object attached to my arms, controlling my movements without my consent, telling me what to touch, how to open the cabinet, when to wipe my forehead, where to search for a sugar cube that I didn't even want to eat. Mundane tasks like brushing my teeth or combing my hair took torturing moments to complete. I felt a disconnect between my brain and my body.

I divided my life into small chunks of time. At first, it was days. One day at a time, that was what everyone advised me to do. Then, as time went by, it was weeks and months. I lived through moments of disarray without showing any signs of sadness to Matthew. I smiled, cooked, cleaned, and tucked him into bed as if nothing had happened. Once he was asleep, I let myself dwell on thoughts that would bring me peace. What if I no longer existed? Was it sheer nothingness that was waiting for me on the other side? What would Keeran say? How would he react? Would he be sorry for what he did? Would he take care of Matthew? What if I told him? Would he come back? Pathetic. Pa-the-tic. When did I get so damn weak? When did I turn into such a pitiful woman unable to get over a broken marriage?

Observing myself from the outside, I started seeing what Keeran came to dislike about me. Tiny love handles disguised behind loose-fitting blouses, lifeless locks of hair, unpolished nails, and dark circles. I looked at me and wondered if that was my 'before' or 'after' look. I couldn't remember.

I forgot what it was like to feel happy. To be happy. I focused so much on my misery that I missed out on so many happiness triggers that I had never ignored before: sunrises over Lake Ontario, an unexpected smile from a stranger sitting across from me in a café, trying on a new fragrance on International Women's

Day as my secret spring arrival celebration, drinking eggnog on a crisp fall night and pretending it was Christmas, writing a birthday card to myself, or modelling Victoria's Secret lingerie in front of the bathroom mirror. Little things that made me *me*.

I had to learn new ways of feeling alive, finding new crutches to anchor me into humanity. I re-learned to be happy and to enjoy small things that hadn't mattered before. That I didn't fall asleep with my winter coat on, I didn't forget to pluck my eyebrows or shave my legs before I showed up for work on a Monday morning, that my cuticles stopped growing, which saved me precious time, that the pot-growing neighbour eventually vacated the house he was renting, that most people whom I encountered during my walks spoke mainly Italian to me, that my favourite Thai dish of green curry chicken with eggplant and sweet basil was now available in the plaza close to my house, that my obnoxious boss had miraculously turned into the sweetest man alive after my divorce, even offering to let me work from home when I needed to.

I kept writing in the journals that Katarina gave me. The weekly blocks of text transformed into landmarks of my new life as a single mom. Some were short, just a few lines, others were longer, going on two or three pages of memories, disparate thoughts, angry monologues, and coping tips that I gave myself on the days when I felt hopeless.

"Ana, how's your writing going? Does it help? Do you find it cathartic?" Katarina asked.

"Cathartic? Now you're getting carried away. You mean journaling. To me, that's not writing."

Sometimes I spent hours in front of the computer, rear-ranging a few disconnected sentences, ending with three question marks as if I had been waiting for an answer, changing the punctuation, switching words around.

I didn't want to tell her that writing had become an obsession. I wrote down bits of conversation, jokes overheard on the subway on my way to work, childhood memories that haunted me, words that I pretended were coming to me in my dreams from shamans reigning over fantastic realms. "Ana, *holstamans ostrrompent voikerd. Hundrs margkcet pribblkt.*" Although I knew that none of those words existed, their healing power was released when I uttered them awake, each consonant and vowel falling into place like rings tossed at a stick in a muckers game. Plop, clonk, plop – their weight reverberated in my ears.

I started eavesdropping on strangers' conversations in the grocery store, sketching out characters based on friends, or simply watching people from a distance trying to read their lips. I fantasized about telling a story without an end, one whose denouement was whatever the reader wanted to make of it. A story about loss, and love, and birth, and darkness, and light. A story built around characters referred to not by name, but by pronouns. Places would also be generic enough to let the reader fill in the void with their own desires: Home, City, Work, Coffee Shop, Office, Destination.

In my never-ending story, I would create a world populated by quiet people, governed by a language that I owned. "*Sodhgin mandter domrrut.*"

I wondered what Katarina would have thought if I had told her I came up with my own system of communication. I decided to keep it to myself. She had already diagnosed me with attachment issues and some other psychological *trauma-schnauma.*

"I don't know, Katarina. I don't know if it helps," I said unconvincingly.

* * *

She gave me a journal every two months. Each cover had a distinctive design: celestial blue with lemon drops, jeweled filigrees, vintage maps, travel stamps, cottage gardens.

"Where do you find all these diaries? Do you run an underground printing business that I'm not aware of?"

"Chinatown. My favourite Toronto neighbourhood. Fill them all up with stories, memories, and dreams. Make it your best friend, one that never lets you down. One day you'll realize your story makes sense the way it is. Don't try to change it. It doesn't need a different ending to make you happy. This is you. This is happy."

"Is Katarina the friend or the therapist talking?"

"Both, my darling," she said, kissing me on the forehead.

I kept writing. Not because Katarina told me to, but because I felt a visceral need to come to terms with my departure, to bring closure to my relationship with Keeran, although forgiveness was a luxury reserved for the confessional. Practicing kindness with Keeran was a divisive topic. He thought people took advantage of me because I didn't know how to set boundaries. *Boundaries-floundaries.* As if I were a piece of land, a country whose borders you could not cross unless you had a permit.

Despite my initial reluctance, I filled five diaries over the course of twelve months. Writing became my escape. It was the first thing I did in the morning, sipping my coffee, and what ended my day. At the beginning, words didn't come out the way I wanted. Awkward, repetitive, sentimental, boring.

I wasn't a writer. I didn't know how to tell stories. Or write them. But I kept going because I could feel the liberating effect of truncated narratives, fragments of life that I wasn't yet ready to share with anyone, imperfect moments that defined me in the present.

Words haunted me my entire life. I over-interpreted people's gestures and conversations. It was a major source of discord between me and Keeran. He always argued that I read more into what he said and that was why I felt so unhappy. My inability to navigate between two diverse cultures that ruled our lives was a constant source of disappointment. Travelling between two countries and two languages accentuated my abrasive nature.

I wrote about the nights when Keeran and I explored the tiny stores in our neighbourhood, browsing through eclectic collections of Eastern European, Middle Eastern, and Western fashion items displayed on mismatched racks and shelves, managed by over-enthusiastic newcomers for whom each customer interaction was an opportunity to practice their English.

One night we entered a store whose windows were plastered with colourful posters announcing a *big selling*.

"*You like?*" a tall woman with a Russian accent asked me when I pulled out a knitted cardigan with faux pearl buttons. "*Try, try, iz good for you. Like colour? Iz good. Try. Reduce. Twenty percent. You like, no?*"

"No, thank you, I don't want to try it on."

"*No... try, try. No like?*"

"I'll buy it."

"*No try, no buy. Zat's it. You understand?*"

70

The fitting room was a red velvet curtain draped over a rusty rod in front of a champagne gold floor mirror. I kindly thanked her as she was peeking behind the curtain to comment on how the sweater looked on me.

"*Looky good. Yes? You like?*" she said.

I left the store with two cardigans in a Loblaws grocery bag that the cash register lady handed out to me smilingly.

As my loyal partner in our shopping excursions, Keeran was delighted at my patience in dealing with people from such diverse backgrounds and, in his very serious voice, declared me *the intercultural queen of hearts*. Each of these adventures ended with a good laugh and basil chicken fried rice at our favourite Thai bistro, a small family restaurant where three generations of Thai Canadians busied themselves around five small tables.

I wrote about the sleepless nights, about the time when Keeran started showing the first signs of doubt about our marriage. Projects at work got busier and more important, customer dinners more frequent, travel assignments more regular. The few nights when he was home early, he didn't join me in Matthew's bedtime routine.

"Ana, I don't know how to bathe or swaddle him. Seriously, I would just be a nuisance. I know you can do it much better on your own. Besides, I have work to finish," he said.

I loved him. And I believed him. Why would I not have? Wasn't he the one who chose me? He wanted to have a family with me. From all the girls he knew, he picked me. Someone who, at job interviews, had to explain where Romania was on the map, someone who didn't know the meaning of double-double when she arrived in Canada, someone who constantly lived between two worlds. He loved that about me.

Or, at least, he used to. My insecurities around my newly formed identity as a Canadian, my linguistic and cultural blunders, my exhilaration at buying Margaret Atwood's *The Edible Woman* in an obscure bookstore in Toronto, my endless questions about what made Canada unique.

"Ana, that's what makes you authentic. You are special to me," he had said on one of our first dates.

I didn't know how to be special. Being myself in a new world was already too much work. Not with him, though. He had a talent for putting me at ease and teaching me how to embrace all of myself. When we were together, I didn't have to censor myself. And that was the best gift that he gave me. After Matthew.

Love is not enough

"Katarina, why did Keeran leave me? Am I difficult to live with? Am I such a horrible person?" I asked Katarina the hundredth time during one of our walks.

"Okay, here's the deal. I know you don't want to do therapy for whatever bullshit reason you want to invoke, but trust me, it would help. To answer your question, or questions rather, no, no, you are not. How does that make you feel?"

"Even worse. At least, that would have given me an explanation."

"Why don't you ask him? It's been a while, both of you have moved on, I mean, I hope you have. I know the breakup hurt a lot, but now you must put that behind you and bring closure to your relationship."

"Okay, that sounds *therap-ish.*"

"Wha-a-at? That's not even a word. What am I saying? Of course, I know you know that's not a word. I mean you're afraid to face your own fears."

"Okay, okay, I know, but this is such a cliché that it makes me ugh, gag. All right, all right, I'm afraid. But what do you want me to do? What should I do?"

"As I said, you should ask him out; go somewhere nice, have a lovely dinner, like two responsible parents of a wonderful child, and talk. I know I make it sound easier than it really is, but it's worth trying."

A couple of days after that, I called Keeran and asked him if he wanted to get together.

"I would love to. Just tell me when and where," he said.

Just like that. No questions asked. He agreed to meet. With me. He let me pick the time and location. Me. Whom. He. Had. Left. For. Someone. Else.

On my way to the pub on Queens Quay in Toronto, I prepared a whole speech on why I thought we shouldn't have split up, on how we can still get back together, or how we could have made things work. Make things work? What was I thinking? What things? Had our marriage been a device that needed repair or just oiling to stop the squeaking? Nothing was going to be the same. How could I have been so blind and not see how different we were, how embarrassed he was with me when we went out?

"What Ana's trying to say is… What my wife means is that…, right, honey?"

Nothing I said or did was good enough, perfect enough for him, for his family, for his friends who constantly judged me.

"Where did you get your information from? Why do you believe that social inequality leads to violence?" They would interrupt me every time I was trying to speak.

"You're wrong. Are there any studies substantiating that? Sorry, no offense, but I've never heard anything so preposterous," someone else said.

As I reminisced about those social events, the idea of giving a speech was as bad as milking an ox. Instead, I decided to show up, sit quietly at the table, and let him do the talking. But not before I asked him why we broke up.

Surrounded by an eclectic mix of furniture and salvaged décor items, I enjoyed the Mediterranean snacks, while Keeran told his story.

"I really loved you, Ana. I did. I know you never liked my parents, but that didn't matter to me, even though I teased you about you not getting along with my mom. And I tried. Very hard. I don't know if you felt the same, but, regardless of how close we got, there was always a bridge between us that you never let me cross. It was your lack of trust. Unnoticeable at the beginning, but more acute as time went by. You left me on the other side. You didn't give me a chance," he said.

All I could hear were words, sounds that came from his side of the table, accompanied by small gestures like a flutter of wings interspersed with a tilted head or a palm side up. Flap, flap, flap. I sat there and I listened. Some of his words reached me like freezing rain on bare skin sending a shock through my body; others dissolved into the air.

I left without saying good-bye.

"So, how did it go?" Katarina asked me when she found out about my meeting with Keeran.

"The food was good," I said. "And the wine."

"That's not what I asked. I don't care about the food. What did Keeran say? Well, forget it, I don't want to know what he said, but I want to know if you got what you wanted."

"Yes, I did. Let's leave it at that."

"Okay, then it's time for you to move on," said Katarina.

"Move on? I like it where I am. I need time."

So, he did love me. But in the end his love wasn't enough.

* * *

Keeran hated my disorganized style, how I hoarded Matthew's drawings, crafts, and quizzes that he started in junior kindergarten. To me, those were mementoes of a life that fulfilled me, substitutes of the pictures that we rarely took as a family and the keepsakes that I rarely received from him on Mother's Day.

Matthew's tiny desk was always messy; piles of Dr. Seuss books, crayons, scented pencils, glitter markers, dollar store plastic toys left over from shoddy loot bags, math sheets, erasers. After months of quibbling, I decluttered it. Sifting through all the items left on the desk that day, throwing everything in labeled buckets, sliding them into shelves that looked like kindergarten furniture. The next day, Matthew couldn't find anything. He wasn't used to having his desk so tidy. Then his desk was left in disarray for several months. After that, the arguing continued so Keeran's neat freakiness won.

When Matthew and I moved out, I gave the desk away. The dinner table became the pièce de resistance in our house: the most versatile piece of furniture that served our needs. We used it for almost everything: eating, playing cards, working, doing homework, watching movies on the laptop, reading.

One weekend, when Keeran came to pick up Matthew to take him to a Blue Jays game, we were sitting at the dinner table playing Rush Hour. A fun game that Matthew enjoyed playing because of the increasing challenges of figuring out how to navigate your car through a traffic jam. I noticed Keeran's frown when he glanced at us: forty puzzle pieces were laid out on top of the table runner in the shape of a cross.

"Hi, buddy, are you ready?" he said, stroking Matthew's hair.

"Dad, let me finish this level, please," Matthew said.

"How long will it take? You know it's a long drive."

"Only a few minutes."

He sat down and waited for Matthew to finish. We never talked when he came to pick Matthew up. We had nothing left to say. Words meant nothing. We used them to express our love for each other. And then our hate. The same words that we used to rock Matthew to sleep when he was a baby were the words that we wrote in our separation agreement. We no longer trusted them.

Tiny dots

If silence was indeed a form of betrayal, was I the traitor? Was I as guilty as Keeran for our failed marriage? I liked to talk things over, while he wanted to give me answers. I expected him to listen, while he focused on resolutions. Our communication pattern was completely unbalanced, creating frustration and resentment.

"Ana, you always complain about your boss Justin. All I hear is problems. If you want to be successful, you need to come up with solutions. No one wants to keep a whiner around," he said to me one night.

When he spoke like that, he sounded like a career counsellor. If you want to be successful...blah, blah, blah. Who cared about that kind of success? He did, I know he did, but I defined success in different terms. To me, relationships were more relevant and meaningful than a pat on the back from my neurotic boss. Keeran instead valued accolades and financial rewards more than anything. Any type of recognition that boosted his ego gave him an opportunity to point out the differences between us: my lack of ambition, my contentment with family life, my background.

I never defended myself, but over time I came to dislike his patronizing indifference. Did he ever try to understand what it was like for me and how I felt?

What he liked about me was also what drove him crazy. It drove us apart.

"Ana, you need to learn how to trust others. This paranoia about people's malevolent motives must stop. You no longer live in Communist Romania," he said.

"I know that, thank you. I don't need you to remind me."

The constant skepticism was an obstacle to my survival in a world where everyone was kind and open in a way that I hadn't experienced before.

I hated his judgmental attitude toward most of the things I said or did, his superiority complex in dealing with people, including me, his lack of empathy in trying to understand how the place I came from had shaped my behaviour, his awful listening skills, his selfishness in keeping his 'me time' sacred, and above all I hated his mother. Her nagging, her condescendence, her discontent when he talked about our marriage.

"Mommy, do you love me?" Matthew asked me every night before I put him to bed.

"Yes, honey. *Te iubesc.* To the moon and back."

"Do you love Daddy?"

"I do."

"To the moon and back?"

"Matthew, it's late. You should go to bed now. We'll talk about this tomorrow, okay?"

Speaking Romanian to Matthew was my only refuge, it was like going back to my own childhood, when my parents tucked me in and kissed me good night. It was a feeling of familiarity that Keeran had never given to me. Speaking my own language, sharing words and sounds that were meaningful in a way that only I could understand.

"You should stop speaking Romanian to him. He'll grow up having an accent and everyone will consider him just another immigrant like you."

"Why does that matter? And why would that be a problem?"

* * *

Katarina offered advice every time we met. There were times I didn't want to hear any of that.

"Honey, do you know how many clients come to me every day? At least ten. Do you know how many of them admit to having relationship issues? None."

"But… I don't understand. Why?"

"Well, you are the best example. Did you speak with someone before you and Keeran decided to part ways?"

"Hmm, I spoke with you."

"Yeah, I get that, but it's different. I'm your friend, not your therapist. Let me write this down. I do that with some of my clients. Write down everything about their concerns, about what makes them whole or what causes cracks in their relationships."

I watched Katarina covering a sheet of paper that she took out of her attaché case that made her look like a KGB agent.

Her writing resembled an abstract painting. With large strokes, she wrote family, love, happiness, child, man, woman, and then drew shapes and lines that connected them to other words that she said were associated with feelings, places, memories, aspirations that she thought might define me. I watched her in silence; her long manicured hands caressing

80

the paper in a continuous motion, hardly leaving its surface. After she covered the page with more words that to me seemed random like flight, worry, childhood, dislocation, loss, sadness, all linked by twisted lines and arrows, she pulled out a pack of highlighters and started grouping them in coloured bubbles.

"Can you see it now? Can you? Do you get it?" she asked.

I didn't. That must have been one of her tactics to take my mind off Keeran.

Much later I remembered her mind mapping demonstration meant to help me understand my story, and how I charted out my life in tiny dots connected by places, names, and words.

C'est chouette

My boss, Justin Côté, was a true Québécois whose love for everything French Canadian equaled only his fanatic devotion to a marketing company that guaranteed him a pension in an economy where fewer and fewer organizations did that. He was on my case from day one when he pulled me into his office and gave me a lecture on how he believed my previous manager had not been highly effective.

"*Mais, oui*, Mrs. Owen, I've heard only good things about you. But you need to understand that I'm not Brian Allington. No offense, I know he was on medical leave before he resigned, but still..."

Of course, he wasn't Brian. I knew that. He was just a nail-biting pathetic man without a personal life, who worked twelve-hour days, had no friends in the office, and moved his desk to face the exit to better spy on our comings and goings.

"I know his type, hands-off, walking around bragging about the results of his team, as if he had a personal contribution. *C'est chouette*, that's cool. *Pourtant, il a été chanceux* to have this group of highly qualified individuals who always make him look good. Yeah, I can give him credit for hiring them. But I'm not like him, no, Mrs. Owen. I don't believe in this hands-off, 'don't bother me' management style crap."

I looked at him with disgust, wondering what kept me there.

"Justin, you know you can call me Ana, right?" I said trying to befriend the monster in a ventriloquist's voice.

"*Mais, bien sûr*, Ana. So, what was I saying? Oh, yeah, that I have a different modus operandi. I expect you to be in the office at eight o'clock, put in your seven and a half hours of work, don't gossip, don't take extended lunch breaks, just be professional, and show some loyalty to this great company."

I took a mental note to roll my eyes when I left his office. Loyalty! What did he know about that? I heard he had changed five jobs in three years before he joined the agency.

"Ana, if today you were to find out that you had only two years left to live, is this really the job that you want to do? That's a big question, a question that I ask all the job candidates during the interview. I'm not saying that's your case. Of course, things are different. You're not just a candidate. I mean you already got the job. You don't even need to answer me now, but I hope you'll think about that."

He stood up, came around his desk, and sat in the chair next to me. He crossed his sausage-like fingers on his chest. His big belly dropped over his navy corduroy pants accessorized with a distressed leather belt, his shoulders slumped under a tweed jacket one size too big. I had to give him credit for the only classy item that completed his attire: a pair of Ralph Lauren shell cordovan leather shoes with hand stitched soles that must have cost a third of my monthly income.

"Ana, my expectation is that for all the projects I lead, you will provide the following: a detailed project plan, weekly updates to both the client and our team, participation in daily progress calls with junior analysts, post-mortem reports, as well as a list of recommendations for the client. Do you have any questions?"

"No, I don't. I've been doing this long enough to know what clients expect, I don't need your reminders.

"*C'est bon*, but you don't know my expectations, *n'est pas*?"

Work, work, work. All the new accounts that he assigned to me were startups. I begged him to give me one that had an established brand; a company that launched a new product or had a sales promotion.

"Ana, we need someone like you for these startups. Do you know why? Consumers' minds are cluttered with super-brands. These entrepreneurs are like immigrants. Moving into a space occupied by so many other companies, they need to be innovative in differentiating themselves from the competition. It's like relocating to a new country where, even though you speak the language, you miss out on the cultural jokes. That's why you can handle these clients so well. *C'est bon, n'est-ce pas*?"

"Justin, I don't know how you got that idea about me. I'm not very creative. I can project manage an account, liaise with the creative director and the copywriter, but I'm not the brain behind their campaigns. I don't know what you've heard."

"*Exactement*, Ana. I didn't say it was you who created the campaigns. I said you were the one who got them where they wanted to be, and you're doing that very well. All the other Account Managers are like stock dogs herding sheep. Don't get me wrong, they are intelligent, but they lack your hunger. In a good way. They just do enough to get by – work off the creative brief, provide minimum input, *et voilà*, their work is done."

"I don't see it that way. Do you know what it's like for an Account Manager to work with one of those iconic brands?

Finding the right spokesperson for the best signature basketball shoes, for example? Or working with a Grammy Award winner to write the song for a TV commercial?"

"Please don't tell me it's like winning the Oscars!"

"Not the Oscars, just an Advertising Creativity Award."

"Ana, *n'exagère pas*. That's ridiculous. These big publications don't even know agencies like ours exist."

I was exaggerating. I thought he was adept at dreaming big. He wanted to grow this business, but he was afraid of what might come out of it.

I knew he had his own protégés – summa cum laude graduates from HEC Montréal, McGill, or the University of Ottawa. I didn't blame him. When I lived in Romania, we had our own implicit bias. We overlooked job candidates with a rural attitude or a regional accent. What did they know about big cities?

"Okay, Justin, forget it," I said.

"Ana, *ne le prend pas personnellement*."

"Why do you think I'm taking this personally? Every time I tell you what I think you say I'm taking it personally."

I didn't need any more hints that he would never let me have one of those accounts. In his mind, I had to earn it, although he didn't put it that way. His discourse on entrepreneurship wasn't anything but a pitiful excuse for his bias. It wasn't like my career depended on it, but I secretly wished he trusted me more.

One day, he came to my desk and said, "From now on, I want you to shadow Melissa, learn everything you can from her because I want you to be her backup. *C'est bon*?"

C'est bon. C'est bon. I knew Melissa Mann was the darling of the office. As a digital strategist, she spent her entire work hours browsing clients' online comments, responding to diatribes, some of them so outlandish that I wished owning a computer or a social media account should be a privilege that people had to earn, like a driver's license or a mortgage.

Although in her late twenties, she dressed like a cougar desperate for attention. Someone who wanted to be noticed. But not in a good way. Though bold, her fashion style was deconstructed and piecemealed, reminding me of a Value Village sale. Leopard print tops, navy khakis, and mustard Puma shoes were her favourite outfits. On the odd days, she would complete her wardrobe with a fuchsia cross-body purse bought at a liquidation leather store in Woodbridge.

"This purse was dirt cheap. *Like*, it had a tiny scratch, so the cashier gave me *like* an additional thirty percent off. Great deal."

She was the queen of store promotions, deals and steals, as she liked to call them. Like a walking red tag library crammed with details about the cheapest places to shop.

Sometimes, her Thrift Store clothes smelled like mold and dust. If you sat too close to her in meetings, you could get a whiff of rotten mangos, tobacco, and moths. A few younger people in the office called her the Moth Lady. Despite her bold allure, she was quiet sometimes, even bashful, emanating a subdued indifference. I didn't get her.

Now and then, she would throw a few words of wisdom at us, neophytes in the social media space.

"Ana, you're *like* a digital immigrant, sorry to say that. I hope you know what it means. No offense there. *Like*, don't underestimate the influence that online communities can have on *like* brands and consumers," she would proclaim from the pedestal of her digital native authority.

The job shadowing didn't go very well.

When I perused social media headlines, I felt judged, conscious of my own inadequacy. Everywhere I looked, I saw posts that promised the Holy Grail of leadership, how to master perfect editing techniques, how to manage difficult employees, or which words to use to look smart. Or not. Formulaic articles devoid of substance attracted hundreds of comments and critiques, making me wonder when all those people found the time to work.

The posts on place or country branding projects always caught my eye. I found it indeed *ESTnoshing* how Estonia captured the essence of its national identity, how the anodyne culture of some place that no one had heard of before, like Kiribati or Nauru, was transformed into flourishing destinations through a discourse developed around a single memorable idea that resonated with people. Storytelling at its best. About the inescapable question of how we decide where to belong. Which place becomes a landmark on our personal journey. Which country defines our identity.

"Ana, you easily fall in love with these concepts, *like*, national identities. But really, there's nothing more creative than, *like*, branding a product. Nothing new here. *Like*, all these consultants and creative gurus, *like*, what they do is apply the same principles, *like*, in branding a product. *Like*, you know what I mean?" Melissa said to me during one of our end-of-the-day debriefings.

I closed my eyes and imagined only the two of us on a deserted island. I pictured how I was going to crack her head open, smoosh the Broca's area of her brain with my bare hands, take the word "like" out, scrunch it up, and put it back in. Then watch her stutter, struggle to find the right sounds, fumble for words, until what came out of her mouth was inarticulate speech, broken sentences riddled with inaudible reverberations.

"Melissa, *like*, no, I don't know what you mean," I said.

The following day, I went to talk to my boss. The job shadowing idea was stupid to start with. He was sitting at his desk, reading a magazine. He didn't even pretend he was busy.

"Justin, this doesn't work for me."

"What do you mean? This what? What doesn't work?"

"This what? What do you mean? This, this, this whole masquerade, this amateurish training, this whatchamacallit job shadowing brain-washing language bastardization social media crap... this freakish girl who... thinks..."

"Stop it, stop it for God's sake. *Ça n'a pas de bon sens*. What the heck does that mean? What does that even mean? What's your problem? I'm trying to help you. *Écoute-moi*, it's good for you to learn what Melissa does. She's the only one with this kind of expertise."

"You call that expertise? When did you lose your common sense?" I said.

"Let's take a break from this. Obviously, you're not interested in advancing your career. I was wrong about you."

"And how exactly do you see that happening by asking me to work with ... her?"

"Her, her? You can't even say her name? *Les femmes... les femmes me rendent fou*. I'm telling you. You two are driving me crazy."

He stood up and walked around. He went to the window, hands crossed behind his back. He paced his office up and down, then he sat down next to me.

"I really want to help. You have great potential. It's your choice if you want to do it."

"You never told me it was my choice. If it is, then I choose not to spend my time listening to Melissa's bargain hunting stories or her pseudo-scientific expositions of digital storytelling. I'm done. Find another guinea pig," I said.

He just sat there. I watched him sinking back into his chair, eyes closed, hands resting on his lap.

I stormed out of his office and went for a walk to cool down. That was when I discovered a park, two streets away from the office.

A portico led you into a gazebo-like structure that housed a monument dedicated to newcomers who had invested in the community. Beyond that, a tennis court and a baseball field that attracted hordes of teenagers from the nearby high school were flanked by a wooded area and a pond, which brought a pleasant breeze to the place.

I sat on a bench and eavesdropped on the conversation between two men in their mid-seventies.

"Are you taking vitamin D? I'm taking vitamin D. Do you know which kind? The 100mg. That's what my doctor prescribed me."

"Oh, yeah? Vitamin D, eh? Maybe that's why I don't have any energy. Going up and down the stairs is a chore for me, you know. I can drive for only forty minutes at a time. It's exhausting."

"Where do you live? Do you want to come over to my place after this?"

"Yeah, why not. I'm not tired. I went to bed at eight last night. My son said, 'Dad, are you sick?' Kids never get it, right? Even when they grow up. It's like they never learn. They don't see us anymore."

They looked at me and I nodded, as if their story had resonated with me, and I felt their loneliness like a rivulet of sadness trickling down my throat, choking me.

Was the agency the right place for me? Endless meetings that we used to call client discovery rendezvous. One time I disagreed with the presenter, a self-absorbed executive. My boss flipped out. Why did they think that marketing to children was ethical? I could not count the times when I sympathized with desperate parents trying to calm down their two-year-olds who threw a tantrum at the cash register because they wanted the candy, or the snacks strategically placed next to the conveyor belt. My disagreement was like a slap in the face, which my boss tried to downplay saying that "I didn't understand the local market."

We won the business, but they decided not to let me manage the creative work for that account. I didn't care.

The park that I had discovered became my secret hiding place. Eating a sandwich in silence, writing in my journal, watching the kids playing ball, eavesdropping on seniors sharing their life stories.

"Ana, you know you're the only one around here who takes a full hour lunch. All your other colleagues cannot afford that luxury. Do you know why?" my boss asked me one day.

"Maybe because they don't want to?" I said.

"Merde, Ana. *Fais-tu expres*? *Tu ne comprends absolument rien*!" he said.

I didn't understand anything? He thought I didn't understand anything?

That was the day when I left his office and didn't go back.

A web of hope

Katarina had told me about an organization that offered settlement services to immigrants and refugees: Settle 4 Less. Run mostly by volunteers, it helped newcomers to adjust to their new life in Canada.

After two interviews with the executive director, a retired high school teacher who had been Katarina's client, they hired me to design and write their leaflets and ESL course materials. I met people who had experienced first-hand the atrocities of war, torture, discrimination, corruption, and political uncertainty. Some had fled their home countries for fear of persecution, watching self-proclaimed democracies dying in darkness and horror. Others left their country in search of a better life. They were all absorbing every tidbit of information with the insatiable hunger for knowledge of middle school students. They sat in their chairs for hours, eyes transfixed on the presenter, as still as human statues that I often saw at street carnivals.

They asked few questions and took lots of notes in their own language – Albanian, Creole, Punjabi, Spanish, Soninke, Uighur, Farsi – a palimpsest of human stories strewn together by a common desire to be safe, to feel at home. When they wrote, they covered their pads with their elbows as if they had been writing an exam and didn't want anyone else to steal their narrative because they were the only ones entitled to chronicle their own lives.

It was a mixed group of people of all ages, different ethnicities. They were coming in small convoys like trailblazers on a snowy mountain, resolute in their pursuit. And, one by one, they took off after the basic language and culture orientation classes ended.

Some of them kept coming back to ask for more advice. We called them *The Comets*. Always on the move, never satisfied, always critical, always asking the same questions – "Some people say 'me, too' and others say 'you, too'. Which is correct?" Others came back with thank you cards made by their children out of construction paper and decorated with dollar store felt and foam toppers. We called those *The Stars*. Sunny, easy-going, happy. They got jobs, continued their education, and felt more Canadian than others, proud of their adopted country.

After they settled in, some of the new Canadians whom we helped also asked us to join them on shopping trips for furniture at The Brick, Leon's, or IKEA. The highlight of their wander through IKEA aisles was the cafeteria lunch where they savoured the meatballs and ate what we called "furniture cookies".

Watching young families holding their kids as they strolled among leather sofas, reclining chairs, and bunk beds, was, to me and my colleagues, a chilling reminder of how fortunate we were. Some of our protégés were as young as twenty-one and as old as fifty-three – two opposite ends of the age spectrum connected like conjoined twins sharing one heart.

One family from Nigeria – mother, father, and four-year-old twin girls – kept asking me for advice on anything they purchased, especially furniture and home décor.

"Miss Ana, which bed we get?" they would ask. "We have not enough money. We not want to buy cheapy-cheapy things. Cheap break easy, no?"

"It depends on what you like. You're right about buying cheap items. It costs you more to replace them because they are not meant to be durable."

"Miss Ana, you like couch? Red couch, like Canada flag. Red maple leaf. What you think? We want red, like Canada. You like?"

"Red is… bold. Yes, I like it, but it's not about what I like, it's about what best suits you and your family."

"Yes, yes, family is important. Miss Ana, you have family?"

"I do have a family, but let's focus on what you need to get done. Write down on that piece of paper the aisle number for each piece of furniture and then I'll help you pick it up on our way out."

"Yes, yes, I do. You show, I know what to do. Thank you, thank you," the father would agree to everything I said.

As far as advice went, my presence was more for psychological support rather than for asserting my authority in matters related to their new life in Canada. They were the ones who helped me by showing so much gratitude for just being in this country, and for including me in their family decisions.

Other families asked me to accompany them on various errands such as dropping off clothes at the dry cleaner's, booking medical appointments, doing grocery shopping, opening a bank account, or signing a property rental contract. Each of their experiences taught me something about their struggles that were not any different from my own after I had landed in Toronto. The language barrier, the fear of falling victim to fraudsters, the job interview anxiety, or the helplessness in front of store cashiers who unmistakably asked too many questions before scanning your produce.

Then, there were those families who wanted our opinion on which sport their children should play or which school to attend.

"Miss Ana, you think kids make fun if son plays cricket or soccer? No hockey or baseball?"

"Give your son options and let him decide. You shouldn't care about what other people think. Kids are more selective than we like to believe. You'll see that your son will develop his own passion, if he's meant to play sports. Just give him time."

"Miss Ana, I want kids go private school. My friends say is best for them."

"Did you go to a private school?"

"No, I go public school when I was kid."

"Only you can decide what's best for your kids. Don't let others influence your choices. Do your research, talk to other parents, but make your own decision based on what suits your child's personality and learning type," I said.

"I want kids go public school, but no gifted program at school in neighbourhood."

"How old are your kids?"

"Four and five."

I recognized in their questions a pattern of what my boss called "accelerated adjustment". Lifestyle choices based on what others within their community did, disregarding their family idiosyncrasies. They were so anxious to blend in that they quickly renounced their traditions. It was a cycle that most new Canadians went through, at least that was what our

Executive Director told us during the onboarding training. With the passage of time, they gravitated more toward their ancestry, celebrating holidays and values that made them stand out.

Working with them was like teaching a baby how to walk. Wobbly at first, unsure of their own moves, they would soon let go of our hand and take the first steps into a web of hope.

Ubuntu

My work at the settlement agency wasn't as glamorous as I liked to believe. The volunteers were genuinely altruistic and believed in the higher good, but some of the employees were so prejudiced that I wondered why they were there.

Ironically, the receptionist, Gord, was so chauvinistic that I questioned how long it would be until someone complained. I knew that kind of attitude would eventually affect the agency's reputation.

"Ana, most of these immigrants and asylum seekers are like rescue dogs. Grateful for a piece of bread falling from our table," he said.

"You're wrong. You're so wrong. How can you be so ignorant? You come to work flaunting your white man privileges like a trophy. You don't know anything about these people."

"I don't? I don't? Well, believe me. I know better. I have this lawyer friend. He takes on a lot of cases. Did you know that many of them have a criminal record and they lie in their application? What do you say about that?"

"How did you come up with that? That's bullcrap. I don't know who your lawyer friend is, but I wouldn't trust him, anyway. How does he win his cases? Let me guess. How does he know these people are lying? You know what they say, it takes one to know one."

"Oh, well, suit yourself. I know you're an immigrant, too, but I wasn't referring to you. I was talking about these people who come to our office. They are from all over the place. Mostly asylum seekers. From Somalia, Nigeria, Guatemala, Colombia, Pakistan, Senegal, Ivory Coast, Mauritania, Mali. Look at them. Feeling entitled, asking for their files to be expedited, expecting social assistance, untruthful in front of immigration officials. Someone should tell them where that money comes from, because I bet, they have no idea. It comes from people like us, you and me, people who work and pay taxes. Yes, that's right. My lawyer friend told me they have no clue. They just come here because they've heard life's better. Of course, life's good when you don't need to work, and money gets deposited into your account every month. You know what we should do? Fingerprint them at the port of entry and send them back if they have a criminal record. That's right. Don't look at me like I have two heads."

He went on and on about how all those people ruined the Canada we knew. How our prime minister was so lenient, building his personal brand on a compassionate discourse that benefited his party, letting down the very citizens who bled red.

I heard there were some cases of fraudulent applications, but I knew most of those people who claimed asylum had fled conflicts, wars, persecution. Some of them, successful entrepreneurs in their country, had lost everything, and came here to build their business from scratch. How could I not admire them? For not giving up, for pursuing their dreams in a foreign land, for embracing a world of possibilities.

Gord wasn't a bad person; he was just in the wrong job. He should have joined a political party to design their election flyers with pompous messages devoid of substance, fighting to keep the status quo, maybe even building walls along the border to keep immigrants and asylum seekers out.

Although I was in a way my own boss, and I loved working with newcomers determined to make a new life for themselves, I found the environment too toxic. Instead of focusing on my projects, I constantly found myself wondering how Gord had landed there, speculating whether other people in the office shared his opinions, doubting that our efforts would be successful.

One day at lunch I called my former boss Justin Cote.

"*Mais, oui,* Ana, *bien sûr, je me souviens de toi.* How are things?" he said in an unusually jovial tone.

"Hm, good, good. I mean, not bad. Hm, how are things at the agency? Any new clients?" I said.

"We're about to land a huge project. Fast-moving consumer goods. I can't share any details," he said.

"Anyway, hm, okay, maybe we can get together for lunch or coffee. Let me know," I said.

"Sure, *ce serait bien.* Email me," he said and then hung up.

Why was Justin so nice to me? What if I made a mistake leaving my marketing job? Maybe Justin Cote wasn't such a bad boss, after all. He had his quirks all right, but didn't I have mine? Wasn't that what I wanted to do? How did I end up working at the settlement agency? I wasn't even the social activist type, nor the starving idealist. Besides, I was slowly developing symptoms of compassion fatigue that all people who worked with highly emotionally charged cases did.

One day, I told myself I wasn't going to be the heroine of these amalgamated stories of abandonment, rebirth, and hope. I did care about those people, but I somehow lost my way amid humanitarian crises unfolding in front of me. So, I decided I was going to remain a pawn in the corporate world finding solace in the few brand naming projects that challenged my linguistic abilities.

A few weeks after that phone call, I emailed Justin and we agreed to meet at the School. A cozy restaurant in Liberty Village, it was popular for its award-winning brunch and their restored industrial space. We lined up at 10:30 am and waited for about an hour to get a table.

"Ana, do you want to come back? With this new client coming on board, I will need someone with your experience," he said.

"Hum, oh…I mean, wow, ugh, okay, yes, okay. Yes, I want to come back. Thank you," I said.

"Deal. Let's enjoy our meal and talk through all the details later, c'est bon? Now tell me about your work. What exactly are you doing at the settlement agency?"

I told him about the people I helped. People stripped of dignity and self-worth. Some of them crossed two continents on foot to find a safe place. They came to our office to tell us their stories. Stories of despair, refuge, and hope. And then they sucked us into their journey, which made us feel lost, too.

* * *

"You're leaving? Why? I thought you enjoyed working with newcomers, helping them settle in," the executive director said when I told her I was considering going back to the marketing agency.

"I do, I really do, but…I don't think this is for me. I get too attached, no, not attached, that's not the right word. Too… involved in their stories. When they come in, I ask them a few questions and, as soon as they open their mouths, I see how rivulets of tears trickle down, merging into a dripping stream on their chin. The crying, the madness, the anger, the anxiety. I've had enough of that," I said.

"I didn't know their stories affected you so much. With some people, you must work on their empathy level, coach them on how to be more empathetic. With you, I'm afraid I have to do the opposite, which is more difficult. But I won't try to keep you here if you don't want to stay," she said.

They threw me a farewell party in the office, with balloons and a thank you card signed in Yoruba, Toishanese, Igbo, Hakka, and Wolof by our clients who also brought their families along, some of the women dressed in Aso Ebi to honour my departure. Souvenirs kept from their trips back home turned my desk into a miniature Dakkar market: silk scarves, hand-made jewelry, carved wooden statues, and tribal masks. A strawberry shortcake decorated with the Canadian flag took centre stage in the group pictures that I promised I would frame. I didn't expect that much attention. I felt ungrateful for leaving behind so many people who accepted me in their lives, who shared with me details about their own dark history, and hoped I would be part of their settlement journey until the end.

I took three days off before going back to the marketing agency. Justin had promised me I would be able to work from home when or if I needed, so, knowing I had that flexibility, I felt urged to show him I was committed to making it work. Between us.

On my first day back, Justin introduced me to a couple of new hires, and then gave me an office. It was undeniably an upgrade from the 6' by 6' cubicle that I had before, squeezed between three shoulder-high dividers that made it look like a solitary.

Something had changed in my boss's attitude. He was more accommodating, less impatient, and over-protective. At meetings, he defended me in front of opinionated jackals who wished to rip my presentations apart. When he went out for lunch, he asked me if I wanted to join him. If he heard me cough or sneeze, he worried about my health.

"You don't know?" Mira from the accounting department said one day. "His wife left him."

"What? She did? How? When?"

"On their tenth wedding anniversary. He told us. He went home after work. With flowers, champagne, and a pair of clustered stud earrings. Diamond. Three carats. When he arrived, the house was empty. She took everything. She left her wedding band and the engagement ring on the bare kitchen countertop. No letter. No phone call. She simply vanished. Since then, he has turned into a huggable teddy bear that everyone loves. He couldn't return the earrings, so he keeps them in a safety deposit box at the National Bank."

After I heard the story about his breakup, I looked at him differently. Maybe he did turn into a teddy bear, but I also reconsidered my options, and I realized the agency was the place where I felt at home. As much as I liked working with new Canadians, pulling multiple strands of their narrative into a much-anticipated resolution, I couldn't do that forever.

The first two accounts that Justin assigned to me were in two completely new industries: automotive and fast-moving consumer goods. The brand managers were fresh Management & Marketing graduates – sharp, ambitious, over-confident. Their creative briefs were dry, academic, openly biased – "no Asians or Latino in this commercial" – and quite removed from the real business world. I learned how to read beyond pretentious paragraphs that sounded like college textbooks and give them credit for the final product. I minimized the stress in my life; they maximized their egos. It was a win-win.

Now and then, I would get a call from clients whom I had helped at the settlement agency. Eguono and Mobo, a refugee couple from Nigeria, used their daughter, Ugoulo, as an interpreter. They wanted to know if I was happy. They never asked about my work, or how much I made.

"Are you happy, Miss Ana? Are you in a happy place? Did you find Ubuntu?"

Did I find the sense of humanity that would ultimately restore balance in my life? Although they explained the translation of Ubuntu as kindness or humanity toward others, they used it in its ancient meaning of "I am, because you are."

I remembered them on their first visit to our office. Wearing their traditional *agbada* and *gele*, smiling, bowing. They looked content. I wondered why they had come here. When I met them, my knowledge about asylum seekers was so limited. It took me time to get to know them, to understand why they were forced to flee their home country. I learned about their village that was set on fire, and how the screams of neighbours trying to escape still haunted them on arctic nights in Toronto. Their serene demeanour, despite the darkness that overshadowed their past, was the only memory I wanted to keep.

Was I in a happy place? Did I find Ubuntu? Eguono and Mobo reminded me of my loss, as much as they reminded me of how fortunate I was to live among people who constantly looked for the good in others. I was, because they were.

Forest therapy

I discovered forest therapy by accident. On one of our hikes in Erindale Park, Katarina told me about a patient of hers who left the corporate world to become a forest therapy guide.

"A what? Forest therapy guide? That sounds like someone who goes out into the woods to apply tourniquets around wounded trees or bandage wilted plants attacked by fungi," I said.

"Something like that. No, no, sorry, I'm kidding. This patient of mine, Kathy, attended a week-long training in California, then she went through a mentorship program with a local guide at Rattlesnake Point Conservation Area in Milton, I don't know for how long, not sure. Anyway, she left her job at a Swiss investment banking firm in downtown Toronto for a life of mindfulness and outdoor living. She offers guided tours in conservation areas and local parks," Katarina said.

"Why would anyone want to go on a guided tour? What is forest-bathing anyway? I don't get it," I said.

"I know it sounds so simple and bizarre, right? Tell you what. Let's try it together. What do you say? It shouldn't cost more than fifty dollars," she said.

"What? I have to pay? There's no way I'm going to pay someone to guide me through a trail. What is she going to give me for that money? Water from the fountain of youth? Or maybe the elixir of life?" I said.

"Now you're being nasty. That's the side of you I don't like. You're so unreceptive when it comes to trying new things. Let's make a deal. I'll pay. Will you come?" she said.

"Okay, I'll come, but you don't need to pay for me. But just so that you know, I'll do it for you, not for your patient turned guide," I said.

A couple of weeks after, Katarina and I drove to Rattlesnake Point to meet Kathy the guide.

"Stop calling her Kathy the guide. Just Kathy," Katarina said on our ride there.

"Okay, okay. Kathy," I said.

We drove for a while. Katarina kept her eyes on the road. I counted the trees and highway signs until exit 320.

It was a week after Victoria Day, the first days when it felt like spring. I woke up to a sunny morning that made me feel grateful for surviving the long winter.

As we drove down the highway, I opened the window to let the fragrant air come in. Blooming lilac trees and forsythia bushes along the road segued our entrance into the park. Drooping chestnut catkins punctuated the landscape.

When we arrived at the meeting point, I could spot Kathy from a distance. When we got closer, I could tell she was one of those women who looked ten years younger. You couldn't have guessed how old she was, or even if you knew for sure, your reaction when you saw her was, "She doesn't look her age." Whatever that age may have been. The fine wrinkles around her eyes stretched into iridescent lines when she smiled. A smile like Venetian velvet spun onto wooden looms. Splendid.

Soft. Secretive. It reminded me of adolescence, insecurity, and unrequited love.

After a brief introduction, Kathy the guide took us and a young couple who arrived late on the tour.

"This is not a hike or a power walk. It's a walking meditation or therapy walk. A chance to feel suspended in time. Open all your senses as you walk through the forest. Feel the earth under your feet, listen to the water stream, breathe in the scented pine needles, touch the leaves, stop and rest your back against thousand-year-old cedar trees," she said.

We walked behind her, no words spoken. A line of obedient followers learning how to slow down, in awe of nature's healing power, silenced by our ignorance.

It took me more than fifteen minutes to start taking everything in. The jagged trunk of the Hackberry Tree felt like a wrinkled crater against my hand; ridges sculpted into scaly bark. The earthy scent of the moist soil tickled my nostrils as I took a deep breath in. The only sound came from raspy vultures lurching over our heads.

We walked for one hour, stopping every ten minutes to participate in what Kathy called connective invitations, guided discoveries of sensory experiences by connecting with nature, being in the moment. The therapy session ended at Buffalo Crag Lookout with an improvised tea ceremony made from foraged chamomile and served in tiny white and pink blossom Japanese cups. Sitting cross-legged with the cradled tea in our hands, we closed our eyes and savoured it.

When everyone finished, we stood up, and walked back in line.

When we reached the parking lot, Kathy gave each of us a hug, got in her car, and left.

Katarina squeezed my elbow before she wrapped her arms in mine. It was a short walk to the car that we had parked at the far end of the lot.

"So?" Katarina asked.

"So? What do you want to hear?" I said.

"How was it? Did you like Kathy the guide?" she said.

"I did. I was wrong about the whole forest therapy idea," I said.

"Good, good," she said.

On the drive back to Mississauga we didn't talk about the tour. Instead, Katarina chattered away about a new patient of hers who was going through a divorce and got into a nasty custody battle with her alcoholic ex.

"Ana, you are the only one whom I tell about my work. I know I'm not supposed to. But I never give you their real names. Besides, it helps me let off some steam. And you're such a great listener. So, this woman, let's call her Bella, believes that her ex hired a private investigator to follow her. I don't know if she's making this up. Why would the guy do that? He was the one who had an affair. Not only that, but he also had some gambling problems. They almost lost the house when she found out. It looks like she's going to win custody of their two boys, eleven and thirteen, so the way I see it, not that I'm a lawyer or anything, but the way I see it, he knows he lost. It doesn't help his case if he hires an investigator. To do what, I ask. Follow a woman whom he no longer loves? Are you listening?" she said.

"Uh-huh," I said.

"Uh-huh what? Did you hear what I said?"

"Yeah, I did. Why are we talking about your patient? I see that some couples are more messed up than me and Keeran."

"Forget it. I'll tell you the story some other time," she said.

After she dropped me off, I took a shower and went to bed.

Forest therapy became my escape. It helped more than Katarina's cognitive behavioural therapy which she offered to try on me once.

"I'll help you identify any negative patterns in your thinking and reframe them into positive behaviours," she said.

"Um, let me see. Hmm, no, thank you. I don't want you to foray into my mind and hyper-analyze every thought I have, any decision I make, every word I use. I would feel naked in front of you."

"Naked? I already know everything about you. "Oh, well, everything there is to know," she said.

"In that case, I'm glad I don't need to explain myself," I said.

"Ana, I want to help. Why don't you come to my office? We can talk. When I'm in my office, I know how to separate a professional conversation from our friendship. Take that out of the equation. I promise you won't be disappointed," she said.

I agreed although I didn't believe that she could help. No one was able to give me a toolkit on how to fix my life. "That's your cross to bear," my mom would have said.

I still showed up at her office on a late Friday afternoon after Keeran picked up Matthew for the weekend. They were going to Charlevoix for the wedding anniversary of one of Devin's friends from high school. As if I cared. He always gave me more details than needed.

Katarina looked very professional. Dressed in a navy-blue suit and a red silk top that matched her flats, she looked like a successful entrepreneur who recently emerged from Dragon's Den. Her office had the appeal of a minimalist living room: a love seat with black finished wooden feet, a cherry coffee table with the latest issue of *Psychology* magazine on it, a writing desk with a mahogany leather chair, a skinny bookshelf, a floor vase with a dry flower arrangement, and an abstract painting on the wall.

"No therapist's couch?" I said.

"No, no couch. I have a loveseat instead," she said.

I sat there for a while before she asked me the first question.

"What is your fondest childhood memory?"

My fondest memory. Why was I there? Katarina was my friend. She already knew enough about me. I couldn't tell her anything more. I didn't want her to be my therapist. She couldn't be my therapist. I didn't trust her separating the two.

I stood up and paced the room, up and down, up and down… I pulled the curtains aside. I looked at the artwork that seemed familiar: an explosion of layered shapes that gave the painting a textured feel.

"Katarina, I can't do this. I'm leaving. I'm sorry," I said.

I picked up my purse and left. I didn't have the heart to tell her that I didn't trust her ability to keep our friendship intact if I was to go through counselling with her.

That was the only time when she tried to take charge.

So, from Katarina the therapist I turned to Kathy the guide. Forest therapy was different. I didn't need to talk to anyone about unresolved childhood issues, or how my father shaped my romantic relationships. All I had to do was practice mindfulness in a serene setting, be kind to myself, and connect with nature – all done my way.

For several weekends after that, I went on guided tours at Rattlesnake Point in Milton or Kortright Centre for Conservation in Woodbridge. On one of those walks, Kathy told us forest therapy or bathing was the Japanese practice of *Shinrin-Yoku*. I liked that. Therapy sounded too clinical, as if we were mental health patients locked up in a fortress.

I learned to take my time and immerse myself in the peacefulness of the forest. I memorized every step on the paths that Kathy guided us on and anticipated the fragrant Canada violets or white honeysuckle shrubs. We never talked to each other. We were always quiet, listening to the brief instructions that Kathy gave us, nodding or letting out vague interjections meant to express our approval or surprise, "Aha," "Hm," "Whoa".

Kathy smiled a lot, but she didn't get close to or share anything personal with any of us. A young couple who always came to the same sessions that I attended were curious about her and kept asking questions.

"Kathy, do you live nearby? How long have you been doing this? What did you do before you became a guide?"

She never responded. She smiled and invited us to observe a leaf or a shrub, run our fingers through the wet soil or hug a maple tree. I could almost taste the sweet, caramelized syrup.

The ritual that I developed included the same outfit, driving the same route, and having the same breakfast that I had on my first trip with Katarina. I returned home with soiled shoes and the lingering fragrance of crushed fir tree buds on my fingers. My cardigan still carried the dust from an odd-shaped rock that I had sat on or the bark of a tree that I rested my back against.

On each outing, I soaked up the experience of feeling connected to nature as Kathy shepherded us along lesser-known trails to avoid the visitor crowds.

After those unencumbered walks, I felt alive, relieved. The anxiety of living alone went away, making room for a new feeling of tranquility that I discovered in solitude.

"You spend too much time with Kathy," said Katarina when I spoke with her on the phone in between two of my excursions. "You've become a *Shinrin-Yoku* fanatic. Or are you obsessed with Kathy?"

"How did you come up with that? You sound upset," I said.

"Upset? Me? No, no, no, I'm not upset. Why would I be? I'm just intrigued by this new passion of yours. Kathy is like an uninvited guest who showed up on your doorstep and you, you, of all people, felt obliged to let her in. Why?" she said.

"What do you want? I don't even understand this uninvited guest thing, comparison, or analogy, whatever you want to call it. Why do you have a problem with me going on these tours? Are you disappointed I didn't accept your counselling? Is that it? I get it. Oh, yeah, I get it. You are. I can see that. But you're wrong. It's not about you or your technique. You are my friend, if I confide in you, I do it as a friend, not as a patient. And I want to keep it that way," I said.

All I knew was that the constant tension I felt in my shoulders and neck was gone, the angst of being a single mom was no longer terrifying, and when I looked in the mirror, I saw a woman whose features I started to recognize.

Je ne regrette rien

Every time my dad called me in Toronto, he asked about all the places that I visited.

"Ana, tell us about your travels. Did you go to Baffin Island? Do you know it's the largest island in Canada?"

He was more interested in what places I had visited than how I was holding up, how my life as a single mom was.

"Yes, Dad, I do know it's the largest island in Canada, and no, I haven't gone there."

But I had been to various places, sharing his dream of exploring parts of the world that sparked his imagination.

"Did you go to Quebec City? Is it true that it's like Paris and they play Edith Piaf? Did you listen to her songs on café patios? You know her songs, right? *Je ne* regrette *rien*?"

"No, I didn't. No one plays her songs there. Who told you that?"

My dad had never travelled farther than the city next to his hometown in the foothills of the Carpathians, a small Romanian settlement known for its Gothic and Romanesque churches that the Saxons had fortified in the twelfth and thirteenth centuries to enable them to stand long sieges, until he moved to Bucharest where he met my mom. The longest trips he had ever done in his life were to an overpopulated school on the outskirts. Although after graduation from high school he took on the breadwinner's role in the family, working in a shoe factory, leaving any personal ambition behind, his love for higher education and faraway places continued to nurture his dreams.

He had never left the country, as the communist regime didn't allow it, but he never gave up on his goal of travelling the world. At least, in his imagination. By the time he had his own family, he had filled up his antique stacking bookcase with an impressive collection of traveller's guides. He organized the thin leather-bound books not alphabetically, but geographically. His favourites were placed on the top shelf, close to eye level, where friends and close family could quietly peruse the titles that never ceased to entice the traveller within him: Paris, Rome, London, Madrid, Lisbon. On the next shelf, the rest of Europe was blending with Asia and Africa, forming a fractured puzzle of exotic places waiting to be explored. North America was on the lower rack, which showed his lack of interest in a part of the world that everyone but him considered the land of all opportunities.

When he was in his late forties, he was invited to give a presentation on France at the local Council of Arts. The call came out of nowhere.

"Ladies and gentlemen, as we celebrate the French Days in Bucharest, I have the pleasure to invite Mr. Adam Sala to the stage, an avid consumer of French art and culture, whose love for *la Replubique* we all share," said the executive director in his introduction.

Not intimidated by the snobbish audience, he took to the podium with confidence, visualizing a make-believe voyage to renowned cabarets, stylish restaurants, and classy bistros in chic areas. That was when I learnt about his fascination with Paris and his love for French music. Everyone loved his flamboyant description of *La Ville-Lumière* that included the cabarets – *Moulin Rouge, Les Folies Bergère* – mentioned the museums *en passant* – *Louvre, Musée de l'Orangerie* – and let the participants' imagination rest on monuments like *Château Versailles* or *Place Vendôme*, while he hummed along with Edith Piaf and Yves Montand, two of the French legends that had performed at the iconic cabaret.

The stories that my dad mesmerized me with before he tucked me into bed at night were not reminiscent of any of the traditional Romanian fairy tales that other kids would listen to. His were vivid recounts of an enthusiastic traveler absconding to spots in his imagination where no one else had access to.

On long winter nights, when the spicy aroma of freshly baked pumpkin pie filled the room, he sat in his favourite chair in front of the TV and, while sipping his homemade red wine, he taught me conversational phrases in Spanish, French, and Italian. Interspersed throughout his travel stories, the foreign musicality of casual sentences gave an unexpected authenticity to his unconsummated dreams. *No se preocupe, querida. Je ne comprends pas. Quando possiamo riverderci?* I shared his linguistic curiosity by learning how to dream in another language.

He passed on his love of books and reading, teaching me how to immerse into someone else's story to only forget my own, showing me how to enjoy sounding up words in my head and marveling at the artistry of how language intricacies, subtleties, and twists served our purpose of telling a story in a

114

very personal way. I came to enjoy the unexpected amalgam of words coming together in sentences that haunted me for weeks after finishing a book.

I had always been proud of him, of how he effortlessly struck up a conversation with people coming from diverse backgrounds, something I had forced myself to learn. I admired him for his ambition, for never giving up on his dreams of exploring the world.

I continued his dream of travelling by choosing to live seven thousand kilometres away and coming back to visit them now and then, fighting to accept a land that looked less and less familiar.

My parents were absent from my life after Keeran and I parted ways. On the few occasions when we spoke on the phone, they were so detached that I wondered whether they really understood that my life had turned upside down. They rarely asked questions about Matthew and me, and never offered to come and visit us, or the other way around. Until one night.

The light of truth

I dreaded the calls in the middle of the night. I knew they were never good news. This time it was my aunt Valeria.

"Your mom's confused, she forgets things," she said.

It was one day before my mom's fifty-seventh birthday.

"What do you mean? Confused how?"

"I'm not sure, but the family doctor said it might be dementia."

I called Dad to see what happened. He had found my mom wandering through the opposite side of the city after someone called 112.

"How did they know it was her? I mean how did they identify her? Did she have her purse with her?"

"Yeah, she did."

"Hey, Dad, do you want me to come home? Be there with you and Mom?"

"Whatever. Do whatever you want. I don't care."

I wasn't prepared to lose my mom to an illness that took her to a land of the forgotten. What would happen to her? How was Dad going to manage on his own? Maybe this was meant to happen for me to go back. I wasn't sure what to do. For the next month, I read everything I could about dementia, early-onset, symptoms, hereditary components. I read about different types of dementia that took people, young and old, to a place of no memories. I read about vascular, mixed, frontotemporal, and Dementia with Lewy Bodies (DLB). All of them sounded like a siege of the brain that slowly surrendered.

I called my boss, Justin, and went to the office to hand in my resignation.

He wasn't happy. "*Pourquoi pars-tu? Pourquoi fais-tu cela?* I won't keep this job for you. Are we clear?"

When I told Keeran we were leaving, he came to our house to lecture me on how the move would affect Matthew.

"Why do you have to go? Why are you taking him with you? He can stay with me, you know," he said.

"Oh, yeah, and how will you look after him? When you're so busy with your new girlfriend, your new life," I said.

"Well, it wouldn't be easy, but I can do it, I guess," he said.

One of the few arguments I won.

By the end of June, I took Matthew and moved back to Romania.

Some things never changed. Even in 2000, clearing through customs and passport control at Bucharest Airport was as tedious as it used to be ten years before.

Boorish agents asked too many questions, disdainfully sizing me up.

"Ana Owen...so, you live in Canada now," the young agent said.

He took my passport without the slightest trace of amiability, his head down behind the Plexiglas booth. I wasn't sure if that was a question or a statement, so I stood silent, not knowing what to do next other than wait. He swiped it through the reader, turned every page, checked my picture, looking at me doubtfully.

"Ana Owen... that doesn't sound Romanian."

In disbelief, it was my turn to size him up.

"You look different in this picture. Turn so that I can see your profile," he said.

I couldn't decide whether it was his croaky voice or the rudeness of his commands that obliterated the memory of a language I used to love. After a few seconds, he dismissed me with a clank of his Turkish gold bracelet adorning his left hand.

I missed the times when my parents looked forward to my arrival as if it had been the single exciting event left in their lives.

They used to start preparations for my visit a couple of months before, fretting over each tiny detail that might spoil my stay. They painted my room, purchased new bed sheets, dusted off my old books, and even bought me a bottle of my favourite pomegranate shower gel prominently displayed on the cracked wood shelf above the bathroom vanity.

Shopping for bed linens used to be one of my mom's most gratifying experiences. A purchase that I made without too much planning put her in touch with the exploding world of retail in Eastern Europe. She started by checking out all buying guides and websites for advice on what to look for when buying sheets, then she visited at least ten stores to feel the fabric, see the weave and colours available, and compare prices. I didn't know why she did it since she ended up buying the same Egyptian cotton sheets that she preferred for their luxurious softness and luster.

This time I picked up my luggage from the only carousel built in the newly renovated airport and proceeded to the south exit where Matthew and I would meet my dad.

I spotted him in the waiting area dragging his feet in a way that used to irritate my mom, a habit that made him look like an old man even when he was in his early fifties. Slouching forward, he shifted his body weight from one foot to the other, almost sliding on the glossy tiles freshly mopped by the old janitor whose footprints marked her path toward the exit. I knew her; she had been working at the airport for a long time. Her name was Sophia, a neighbour of my parents'.

His crocheted painter's beret tilted to the side exposed his large ears that destroyed his self-confidence when he was a teenager. The Buckingham plaid scarf tied in a French knot fell loosely on the sides of his charcoal wool-blend Forester coat that I had bought for him in Canada the year before.

When he saw us, his face lit up and he started walking faster, trying to lift his feet off the ground, but the effort seemed to tire him out, so he went back to his shuffling.

"Hi, Dad. You didn't need to come and pick us up. We could have got a cab," I said.

"Oh, don't be silly. You don't want to drive with a crabby cabby," he said. "How are you, young man?" he asked Matthew, who gave him an awkward hug as it was the first time they had met.

I didn't find that funny. His sense of humour had always eluded me and almost infuriated my mom every time he would crack a joke at social gatherings. I pretended I didn't hear him. We exited the terminal, heading for the parking, and, as I watched him busying himself with my luggage, I could see how the wrinkles and creases on his face had deepened since my last visit.

Dad smiled at us as he fit our expandable Via Rail suitcases into the trunk of his lime-green Trabant, a car he had bought after the fall of the Berlin Wall through a connection who used to do some engineering work in East Germany. He had never considered getting a new vehicle, as his interests rarely went beyond the simple accumulation of knowledge. To him, education had always been the ultimate bastion of human existence, therefore it was the only investment he believed in.

When I looked at him, I remembered how he used to tell me that a genuine desire to know more would turn me into what he liked to call *homo sciencis*, as if it were a new human species sprouting from ambition or curiosity to defeat ignorance.

"Dad, there's no such thing as *homo sciensis*."

"Oh, I know, I know. I made it up. From the Latin word '*scire*' which means 'to know' and gave us the word 'science'."

In the car, I watched him as he drove down the tree-lined boulevards of Bucharest, the capital city once known as 'the little Paris of the East', a nickname earned because of its architecture and its cultural elite educated in France between the two World Wars.

When we arrived at my parents' house, my mom was sitting in the kitchen. She stood up and squeezed us into a three-way hug. Wrapped up in her favourite apron bought in a souvenir shop in Boston almost three decades before, she looked fragile and diminished.

She was in her late twenties when she went to Boston to meet with a friend who was finishing her Ph.D. in Psychology at Harvard University. The aura of being associated with such a person, heightened by the excitement of visiting one of the oldest cities in the United States, which she was able to do with a special approval from the Ministry of Internal Affairs, was enough to make her heart race. She loved the apron. It was a vivid reminder of her lost youth, of the vibrant memories she refused to share with us, of her intense life before she had me. Unfortunately, the clam chowder recipe that accompanied the apron never found its way into her traditional cooking. The 'minced clam' sounded too exotic for my mother who had a taste for bland foods, and, besides, she wouldn't have been able to find the ingredients in Romania.

My dad had always been the better cook in our family. We used to call him *șeful*, a double entendre he didn't reject: cook and boss.

He liked trying new recipes. When he once tried to talk his brother into taking some cooking classes at a local grocery store, he thought he was going to be stoned to death.

"That's where a woman belongs. In the kitchen. A true man should never learn how to cook. Only a weak man like you would fathom himself a chef," his brother said.

He experimented in the kitchen, mixing up garlic, oregano, zucchini, sun dried tomatoes, and lemon zest. He even created his own recipes treasured in a handmade cookbook proudly exhibited on a wicker shelf next to the stove.

All our family gatherings were intricately orchestrated around a large variety of traditional dishes that I had never attempted to try on my own when I moved out.

"Every time I see you, I remember the little girl who entered the church on Easter Sunday, holding her shoes in her hand," my dad said out of nowhere. "Do you remember?"

How could I forget? It was back in 1982, when we celebrated Easter with my grandparents. It was a Sunday morning in early

April. The earth was slowly coming back to life after what had seemed like an endless winter, with bitter snowstorms hitting the rows of brick houses from the north and wearing down by the time they reached the open fields where farmers had erected rudimentary sheds to store away their tools.

The road to church passed through a vast land of what was to become heavy crops of canola and sunflower, timidly sprouting from the moist soil. I was wearing a new pair of shoes that my parents, in keeping with the family tradition, had bought for me a few days before Easter. Made of black and yellow suede, with rounded toes, they tightened around my ankles with thin bi-colour straps. My knee-length dress was coming down in frills covering up a pair of skinny legs. Layered over my dress, I was wearing a black wool cardigan that my grandmother had knitted in only a few days, carried away by the frenzy of Easter holiday preparations.

The ground was still covered in a thin layer of snow that crunched under my feet like salt crackers. I didn't want to ruin my new shoes, so I took them off and continued my walk. I counted my steps, knowing from the previous years, that it would take me exactly two thousand five hundred and eighty-three steps to get to the wooden church that, since the eighteenth century until recently, had served as a praying sanctuary for the small community that we were living in. Despite the overt efforts of the communist regime to desacralize churches and monasteries, humble attempts of the residents had kept them alive a little longer.

I reached the church, walked up the stairs, and went inside. I stopped by the icon stand and lit a candle. My mom had told me the church was oriented East-West because it symbolized the entrance of the faithful from the darkness of sin into the light of truth. I never quite understood the metaphor, but, as a child, I had come to associate the light of truth with the tons of candles scattered throughout.

To us, Easter carried no significance related to human rebirth or redemption. Living in a country where churches were either demolished or relocated from central boulevards to prevent the few Christians from entering and praying, spirituality unequivocally equated religion, so it was banned from daily conversations, from our daily lives, leaving us empty, but hopeful that, one day, things would get back to normal.

I looked forward to Easter dinner, when our extended family would get together and recount stories of their youth, a past governed by dreams that were never considered out of reach. My parents celebrated Easter with a mix of subdued spirituality and a culinary feast of Romanian dishes.

For the main course of cabbage rolls, roasted pork, and polenta, my parents would work for an entire day before the festive dinner, busy with so many variations of cooking, cutting, dicing, mixing, seasoning, and tasting.

Long after Easter Sunday, our house kept captive smells and aromas that brought the tradition alive, and made us, the younger generation, embarrassed that our moms were not using more sophisticated recipes. My cousin and I avoided the heavy appetizers: deep-fried meatballs made of ground pork, seasoned with fresh parsley, dill, and garlic, homemade hot sausages, and *bœuf* salad. My dad told us the latter dish, although it sounded French, it originated in Russia, invented by a famous chef, Lucien Olivier, and was initially called Salad Olivier, made of diced boiled potatoes, carrots, pickles, beef, peas, and mayonnaise. Over the years, my mom, like most Romanian women, adapted the recipe to her own needs, replacing the beef with chicken, adding or removing ingredients that were not available in the store until the final product carried little resemblance to its origin.

Cinnamon & lemons

Within a couple of weeks after my arrival in Romania, I found a job as an Event Coordinator for a Dutch literary agency that had recently opened an office in Bucharest. I spent my days taking care of my mom, helping Matthew to adjust, and frequent trips to Amsterdam to meet with authors whom we represented in Romania.

As time passed, mom became even more confused. One day, she crouched in the corner of her room, holding her belly as if someone had punched her in the stomach. I could see her tears staining the green bandeau dress my dad had bought for her at a Marks & Spencer store in downtown Bucharest the summer before I moved to Canada. It was the kind of dress that young women would wear, but my mom had always been bold. Besides, she never looked old to me although she kept reminding me that now she was a grandmother.

Another time, she refused to move. I watched her cry. I didn't move either. I stood by the window, waiting for her to finish. I knew the ritual. She didn't want me to speak until she was done. How many times had I seen her do this? I had lost count. I looked out the window, my eyes half-closed. I sat back to enjoy the jewel tone colours of the freshly planted petunias, marigolds, and nasturtiums. My mom had never agreed to spend any money on perennials, she found them too boring.

Although they still lived in the low-rise apartment building that I grew up in, they took advantage of the small plot of land in front of their balcony. Every year she went to her favourite garden centre and brought home a trunk full of annuals. Nasturtiums were her favourites. That year, she could not go. So, I went instead. I bruised my knees, digging in the ground for a whole day.

She was like a small child, my mom. I didn't know what to do with her.

"Mom, the doctor said a terrible illness has eaten her mind. Did this illness get into her head and ate her brain?" Matthew asked.

Dr. Teodor laughed when I told him; he gave me a pamphlet and asked me to be patient. I showed the flyer to Matthew and read to him about the illness that took his grandma to a place without memories.

I knew there had been signs, but no one helped, no one warned my dad how to read them, how to interpret them. No one showed him what to do. Dad told me one day he found the saltshaker in the fridge. Another day, he found her toothbrush in the oven. She kept looking for it all over the house. She did that with me, too.

"Mom, it's not in the bathroom," I said.

"What do you know? You're just a child. I will find it," she said.

No, mom, you are the child, I thought, avoiding her eyes. I was afraid this terrible illness would eat up my mind, too, because sometimes my whole body felt heavy and wobbly, I was forgetting things, I couldn't find my words. Our family doctor said I shouldn't worry; it was the shock caused by the news of her illness. That was my emotional refuge and excuse for appearing scatterbrained. 'It's a shock, you know.'

I wished I could take away her pain, I wished I could see her happy again, laughing through the empty rooms, pulling the curtains away and wrapping them around her, pretending she was a long-forgotten queen shipwrecked on an island inhabited by dreamless daughters like me.

One night she ran away, tramping through the endless night. I called 112 and they helped me track her down. We found her hiding in a makeshift shelter under Grant Bridge, on the east side of Bucharest, in a cardboard tent most likely hastily put together by a homeless person wandering around the city. When I brought her home, I held her in my arms, and, stroking her damp hair, I rocked her to sleep. She was my second child. She was my curse.

Our Polish neighbour, Mrs. Pomirska, watched her when Dad went out and I was at work.

"Come, Lina. Here, here. I make you tea, sit, sit."

Mrs. Pomirska was the nicest lady I'd ever met. When I was a child, she always spoiled me with her homemade sweets – *chrusciki*, fried pastries covered in icing sugar, foldovers or *kolaczki*, doughnuts or *bismarks*, and *makowiec*, a poppy seed roll. I could tell she was baking even before she brought us some of her desserts. I could smell the cinnamon, the fragrant Meyer lemons, the toasted walnuts, the ground poppy seeds. Our balcony was a festival of aromas lingering on the stone tiles, making their way inside through the open windows, pushing through the cracks in the wall, waking me up, alluring me to the neighbouring apartment where the normalcy of living was a given.

My mom had never been a baker. Flour and sugar were never on her grocery list. She used to tell me the only reason why sugar companies continued to prosper was because of immigrants like Mrs. Pomirska. I didn't care what she thought about Mrs. Pomirska's desserts or about her heavy accent. I loved them, and I loved her for being nice to us. No other neighbour visited us after my mom fell ill.

My mom looked confused all the time. She was lonely and forgetful. She forgot to make dinner, going to bed before Matthew, and leaving him stranded in an empty apartment that echoed her suffering like muffled sounds bouncing off the walls.

Burano

At first, Matthew felt out of place. He hardly spoke the language, he didn't know any of my old friends, my parents were like strangers to him. I still hoped he would get used to his temporary home.

"Mom, my teacher said I'm very smart," he said to me one day. "She said that, even though my language skills are not at the same level as the other students, I've made progress quickly."

His teacher, Mrs. Petronia, helped him adjust to the new school. One day, she slipped a ham and cheese sandwich into his bag when they went outside for recess. I knew it was her. Who else would have done that? Matthew said he ate it on his way home, without letting any crumbs go to waste, licking his fingers, stuffing the aluminum foil into the back pocket so that he could smell it at night before he went to bed. Because he knew Grandma would forget to cook. Again.

Once Matthew made a card for Mrs. Petronia – on thick red paper that he picked up from the grocery store. She thanked him with a wink, patting him on the head.

"I wish she was my grandma," he said to me one day.

"Why, honey?"

"Because no illness swallowed up her mind."

That was one way to put it, but my mom didn't seem to get better. On the contrary. It was close to Christmas when my aunt Valeria arrived from Sibiu to help me take her to a long-term care facility. The owners advertised it as a home built for people like her – forgetful, sad, mindless. I hoped she would be happy there, although I would miss her.

We packed up her things, took her medical file from the family doctor, and drove her to Snagov, about thirty kilometres north of Bucharest, where my parents used to take me for daily trips when I was little. The facility was built right by the lake, whose elongated shape reminded me of Lake Ontario. The staff was friendly enough and my mom didn't show any resistance when they showed her to her room.

My aunt asked us to move to Sibiu and live with her and her husband for a while, but I didn't want to. I knew she resented me for leaving Romania, so I avoided getting exposed to endless reprimands, callous remarks, and so-called constructive criticism. Besides, I had a job in Bucharest which I didn't want to lose.

Uncle Petru was an editor for a German magazine, scouting talented writers to help them get published. He used to make fun of me when I sent him interminable letters in which I rambled about the blooming nasturtiums, my silent mom, the heavy-accented Mrs. Pomirska, and the fruity fragranced Mrs. Petronia. He teased me, calling me his favourite writer. I liked that. One day I could write about all that. The empty house. The stifled crying. The bismarks hidden in cupboards. The books in the fridge. The soap in the oven. The silent mother crouched on the floor.

We did go to visit them, though. They lived in the Lower Town, or Unterstadt, in a small German community where most two-storey houses had fortified gates leading into inner courts with cobblestone paths winding between potted plants and hibiscus trees. Their house didn't have an atrium, but they loved it because it was the only medieval feature of the town architecture they didn't like. The exterior of the house was painted rose quartz, with Mardi Gras gold windows, and a Killala green garage door. They had picked the colours after they returned from their honeymoon in Burano, an island in the Venetian Lagoon.

Valeria had shown us pictures of Burano: narrow streets, petite houses punching their roofs through the Romanesque architecture, a rainbow of paints splashing the canal. What struck me the most were the brightly coloured houses yelling at me from each photo. The residents of the small town had to ask for permission from the government if they wanted to change the paint because, my aunt told me, there were strict rules that they had followed since the golden age of the town's development. I never quite understood how someone else could dictate how you should paint your house, but Valeria assured me it was for the benefit of the community, to preserve its history, the charm that attracted so many tourists.

I still remembered her album – packed with glossy photos of odd couples sitting in sidewalk cafés, miniature windows bursting with lavender blooms of Parma violets, clotheslines connected between narrow buildings, winding stone steps descending to the canals. She had chosen the Venetian Lagoon over Figueres, where my uncle Petru wanted to visit the Salvador Dalí Museum.

My aunt used to make fun of those times. When they argued about everything, when even the most insignificant decision they had to make as a couple turned into the Battle of Caudine Forks.

"Valeria, the museum itself is a work of art. It's impregnated with his spirit. Anyone gets it. It's a museum that Dalí himself designed with the purpose of delivering a surrealist experience to everyone who entered it," my uncle said.

"I don't like him. He's too creepy. The melting clocks, his disintegrating self-portraits, the chopped-down *Madonna de Portlligat*, his *El Gran Masturbador*. He had a distorted mind. Sick. Psycho," my aunt Valeria said.

My uncle had stopped arguing with her. After many years, he brought up the idea of going to Barcelona where they could take the train to Figueres. It was only a one-hour ride. She wasn't one to be easily persuaded. She didn't even consider that as a vacation spot. So, my uncle Petru started collecting albums, pictures, engravings, and even Dalí souvenirs sold on eBay that he displayed proudly in his home office, with complete disregard to what his wife thought about his unusual interest. He had stuffed his room with trinkets, letter-size prints, and cheap reproductions of *Port Alguer* and *Leda Atómica*. My aunt disliked them. She felt uncomfortable when her friends' kids were sneaking up into Petru's room to look at the naked woman holding the swan's head in her hand.

"What's up with the book and the egg floating in this picture, anyway?" she kept teasing my uncle.

"Valeria, I told you. It's all about symbols. Besides, Dalí organized his painting following the golden ratio. If you look closely, you can tell how Leda, who's actually his wife Gala, and the swan are harmoniously framed in a pentagon which is included in a five-point star that symbolizes perfection through love, order, truth, determination, and action. The egg alludes to the story of Leda who was raped by Zeus who is the swan in…"

"Oh, my God, Petru, you've told me this story so many times. Where did you read that, anyway? Wikipedia? Please, I know it by heart."

Although they had a happy marriage, they never took each other seriously when it came to discussing their interests. Valeria was stubborn, refusing to listen to anything related to Petru's obsession with Salvador Dalí. Petru wasn't the man to get into a fight over ideas, so he complacently gave in to her whimsical nature, secluding himself in his own world, moved by dreams bigger than Valeria could ever imagine. He dreamed of climbing Mount Everest although he wasn't a climber, going into the Amazon rainforest to live with an Indigenous tribe for one hundred days, and flying a plane over the tea plantations in Tanzania to reach Mount Kilimanjaro. He never did any of these things, blaming his indecisiveness on aging, but he once confessed to me that Amazonia wasn't a far-reaching goal, he would go there someday.

Many times, Valeria found him locked up in his room, listening to Ottmar Liebert's Barcelona Nights on his old CD player, over, and over, and over. Valeria's practical nature didn't give in to his pleas to get an online music subscription, so they still had hundreds of CDs organized on a spiraled wood rack built by Petru's brother, a wood carving enthusiast.

I always wondered why they got along so well despite the apparent disagreements – two contrasting personalities, guarding their desires, releasing their anger, but always coming together as a whole. The invisible thread that joined people into a couple fascinated me since I was a child.

"Mom, did you have another boyfriend before you met Dad?" I remembered asking my mom when I was ten.

She laughed and said, "Yes, I did, but that was a long time ago."

"Mom, how do you get a husband?"

"You fall in love. You just know. It's a special feeling that you can't describe."

"Why can't you describe it? I don't understand."

"Because love just happens," Mom said.

When I met Keeran I remembered what she said. But that was a past life. The transient feeling of connectedness grasping the ineffable essence of love.

Valeria was different. She had none of my mom's spontaneity, of her desire to face a tumult of experiences. A big spender, she had turned into a high maintenance woman who believed she deserved everything. No job was good enough for her. No friends were as cultured as she, no men were as successful as Petru.

* * *

Our stay in Romania wasn't what I expected. I didn't have too many friends. The only people whom I was close to when I was in university had left the country and cut all ties with their families. Forging new relationships in a place that lost its relevance felt like trying to melt iron at freezing temperatures. I met a few editors at book presentations or fairs, but they had their own circle of acolytes, and didn't seem interested in getting new chums.

At the International Book Fair in Bucharest, I met a couple who were running a new publishing house, *Le petit livre de poche*, a local version of the pocketbook, whose ambitious goal was to re-launch paperback books in Romania in a much smaller format and at an affordable price. Miron and Amalia Simpetru had sold their one-bedroom apartment and invested all their money in promoting local writers. Within two years, they had published five books that sold well and allowed them to buy back the apartment. Modest and enthusiastic, they were the opposite of what I expected to see at Bookfest.

"Ana, you can represent our authors in Canada. Wouldn't that be awesome? We can be partners," they said when I told them I lived in Canada and was in Bucharest only temporarily.

"Well…errr… I don't know, I mean, I can't, ahh. This is not what I do for a living in Canada. I'm so sorry. But I can do some research when I go back and send you some information," I said.

"That works, too", they said. "Don't leave without giving us your email address."

People like them made me feel guilty that I wanted to leave. Again. Others, didn't.

"Ana, you have to admit you no longer understand how things are being done here," one editor said. "You keep telling us about Canada. Listen, I'm just being honest with you. Don't try to change the way we do business. Stay away from giving us advice on which books to publish, and we'll pretend your ultra-politically correct, over-the-top politeness doesn't bother us."

Ştefan M. was the Methuselah of the Romanian publishing world, who had retained the old guard leadership style – dictatorial, conceited, chauvinistic. His connection with established authors and political leaders kept him at the top in an industry that was slowly evolving.

People like him made it a moral imperative to lecture me on my uprooted views on how to run a local business or what type of fiction genres would attract readers to book fairs.

"We are the ones who stayed behind," he proclaimed during our encounters. "The ones who believe in changing this country. I know your type. You can't simply show up after all these years and wave your North American experience like a trophy. You don't belong here. Don't you see? Go back to your Canada."

His hired minions echoed his opinions, nodding in silent approval to everything he said. Did I need to explain I wasn't there to change him, them, or anything? That my stay was just a phase in my own reconciliation journey with my family and my past?

Matthew had a couple of weeks left before the end of grade four. The few friends he made at school were not enough to make him feel at home. We both got invited to parties where grownups took over, and kids were left to their own devices, literally. Feigning interest in conversations about Romanians' leadership skills wasn't my forte, so I stopped going. Matthew tried out for the basketball team, but the coach said he was too short, and he should wait until grade five. The school didn't offer any other sports, and I was busy with my mom, so Matthew spent his time doing extra homework, watching CBC Kids online, and Skyping with Katarina about The Living Arts Centre shows that were on that season, the opening of the skating rink at City Hall, and rollerblading through the park along Humber River.

"Mom, I hate it here. No one likes me. Kids at school make fun of my accent. Do we have to stay?" he asked one day.

We didn't have to.

"My friends David and Mihai don't want to come and play with me. I want to go home."

As much as I tried, I felt out of place. Sites that once were familiar no longer carried the same significance, my own language betrayed me in simple sentences that came out awkwardly, with unnecessary prepositions buried in convoluted syntax that even I found difficult to replicate. I did want to go back to my Canada.

One night, I told Matthew we were going home.

"I've had enough. We don't belong here. Let's go home," I said. He jumped on the bed, singing " *Ô Canada!/Terre de nos aïeux, / Ton front est ceint de fleurons glorieux!...*"

Tsundoku

All the years that Matthew and I spent together, without Keeran, came and went leaving few distinct memories. It felt like I woke up one morning and my little baby boy was gone. Instead, I was the mother of a young man whom I discovered in small bits. That he had a girlfriend, for example.

"Who is she? Where did you meet her?" I asked him when he called to tell me he was bringing his girlfriend home for Thanksgiving. When did he have time to meet someone? He had started university less than a year before.

"Her name is Julia Lazăr. I met her in the Biochemistry class. She's Romanian, Mom!" Matthew said victoriously. "She came to Canada as an international student, sponsored by her aunt who lives in Cornwall."

She lived at the Chestnut Residence, only a few minutes away from the University of Toronto St. George Campus, downtown Toronto, where Matthew spent most of his weekends from then on.

He enjoyed the campus life, a kaleidoscope of experiences that gradually immersed him in different cultures. I never asked him what he did when he was there, what kind of people he met, what books he read, what he missed, what he longed for. I was happy he found a place where he didn't have to explain himself.

When he brought Julia home for Thanksgiving dinner, I saw right away why he had fallen in love with her. At five-foot-eight, with heavy auburn hair subtly highlighted, falling in waves over turquoise eyes, she could have easily passed as a model getting ready for a fashion show. I had never seen eyes like hers. Bright blue-green with flecks of honey like liquid gold that looked almost translucent in the sunlight and darkened to teal when she stayed in the shade. She smiled a lot, complimenting me over my dishes. I wondered where she had learned English. Other than a thick accent, her grammar was perfect. I bet she was coming from a well-off family that sent her to private schools in Europe and hired tutors to prep her for secondary studies abroad.

"My mom never cooks turkey," she said. "She doesn't know how to do it. I like the intense flavour of dry and fresh cranberries mixed with seasonings and apple skin. What kind of apples did you use?"

I was surprised to see she knew the different flavours, able to tell with precision what seasonings and ingredients I used for my stuffing.

"Swiss apples," I said.

"Swiss apples? What kind? Do they grow in Canada?"

"No, they don't." I smiled nonchalantly reciting from the cookbook that Katarina had lent me. "This variety of apple, Uttwiler Spätlauber, is quite rare and recently it has even been hailed as an anti-aging panacea. Cosmetics companies are using Swiss apple stem cells to create a cream they claim may be stopping the aging of human cells. I've read that if the bark of the tree or the fruit gets punctured, it heals itself."

139

She just sat there and smiled. In that instant I fell in love with her, too. I loved her genuineness, the way she handled herself in awkward situations. I knew I sounded crazy. First of all, she asked me about my recipe and I, instead of answering her question, started to rattle along about some serum that allegedly made your skin look younger.

"Of course, that's not the reason why I used it. I mean, not for its cosmetic properties. Although it doesn't have a sharp flavour, I like its creamy texture that makes it easy to cook and mix with other fruits."

She smiled again, put her knife down, and raised her glass of Shiraz Cabernet.

"To Ana! Thank you for a wonderful dinner," she said.

Matthew looked at me, raised his glass, seeking my approval before he said, "Thank you, Mom."

I didn't need to tell him that I liked her. Since he was little, we had developed an understanding that didn't require too much talking. Just like my mom, a woman of few words, whose laugh or downward smile gave her away before she said anything.

That night he went back to Julia's downtown residence. I didn't see him for a while although he called me every other day. He made a habit of coming home to pick up clothes when I wasn't there. The first week of December, they called to let me know they were going away for Christmas. They rented a cottage in Tobermory, on Bruce Peninsula.

"Mom, why don't you come with us? It will be good for you." He sounded just like his dad. His invitation wasn't phrased as an affirmation, as if he wasn't sure he meant it. Why would I go with them? I came up with an excuse and neither of them insisted.

When they got back, they came to show me hundreds of pictures taken during their one-week stay. Julia playing in the snow, Julia waking up, Julia drinking her coffee, Julia smiling at the camera, Julia's silhouette in the sunset, Julia throwing snowballs at Matthew or whoever was taking the picture, Julia snowshoeing, Julia skating, Julia....Julia. Only one picture of Matthew eating Korean barbecue and kimchi. He ate what? He never liked fermented vegetables. He never ate Korean food. And I know for sure he didn't like snowshoeing.

"Look, Ana. Isn't he funny? Making these faces, trying to eat kimchi?" Julia laughed, throwing her head backward, stroking her hair with her left hand.

No, he wasn't funny, and no, I didn't like that he was trying foods that he hated.

* * *

"What do you mean he's moving to Romania? What the fuck have you done to this kid? You screwed up his life with stories about this idyllic place that exists only in your imagination. Why would he even want to go there? I can't believe you are okay with him leaving. I can't believe this. Mom was right about you. You're evil. Evil. You and your emotional time warp. Continually haunted by shadows of your past, not able to deeply connect with people, always suspicious of real intimacy. I'm coming over," Keeran said, hanging up on me.

Oh, well, he was coming over. What was he going to do? Give us one of his endless lectures on why success mattered? How I transferred my own unfulfilled ambitions onto Matthew? How I never belonged here?

Matthew was upstairs packing when Keeran rang the door. I didn't bother to answer.

141

"Mom, the door," Matthew yelled from his closet. "Mom, are you there?"

A few seconds passed until Matthew decided to run downstairs. I could hear him from my room.

"Dad...ugh... come in. I didn't know you were coming. Let me get Mom."

"No need. I want to talk to you."

"What's up?"

"Is it true that you're moving to Romania or is this one of your mother's stupid games?"

"Games? What do you mean? And why would you care, anyway? You're the one who left us, remember? Now, all of a sudden, you care about me? Please, spare me. Was that all? Because I'm quite busy. I don't have time for your speech on how I should live my life. So, if you don't mind..."

"Wait a minute! You don't even want to talk to me? How did you turn into such an insolent self-centered ungrateful son?"

"Me, self-centered and ungrateful? I guess, like father like son. You should be proud."

"Matthew, please, listen to me. You're making a big mistake. Do you remember when you stayed in Romania with your mom for a while? You hated it."

"I did, but I was just a kid. Besides, I'm not alone. I'll be staying with Julia. We want to start a family. And Bucharest is not the city that you remember from mom's descriptions. It's buzzing with expats, it's safe. It attracts millions of tourists every year."

"You're starting a family? Who the fuck is Julia?"

"That's another reason why you shouldn't be here. You're no longer part of this family. Our family. You stopped being my dad a long time ago. Now, you really have to excuse me."

I heard the door open and Keeran swearing as he got out. What did he hope to accomplish by showing up like that? Why would Matthew listen to him? He was no longer a little boy, looking up to his dad, absorbing every word, believing everything he heard.

Although I somehow shared Keeran's concern about Matthew leaving, I wouldn't have admitted it in front of him.

In 2013, Matthew graduated with a Bachelor of Science in Chemistry at the top of his class and he already had several job offers lined up: Sanofi-Pasteur, AstraZeneca, and GlaxoSmithKline. All he had to do was choose one. When he went to the interview at GlaxoSmithKline, they told him about opportunities in Eastern Europe with relocation options for Budapest, Bucharest, or Prague. He picked Bucharest, where Julia's parents lived.

He loved Julia. He loved her a lot. More than I had imagined. Otherwise, why would he choose to move to a country whose name he wasn't even able to pronounce until in his teens? I did everything I could to stop him. I put all my fears into him. I tried to scare him, to threaten him, to beg him. It didn't work. He was only twenty-two years old and already made life decisions that excluded me.

After he left, I learned how to make pretzels because Matthew liked them. It also reminded me of this place in Romana Square in Bucharest, where students used to stop by on their way to class to grab a couple of hand-rolled sea-salted or poppy seed pretzels, perfectly baked and served on parchment paper. I specialized in three recipes: sesame, poppy seed, and parmesan herb.

I then ventured into creating my own version of traditional recipes that I hadn't been interested in when I lived with Keeran, craving foods that smelled like my mom's kitchen and brought back to memory a place that was going to be the home to my own son. Grated feta cheese, sour cream, and hard-boiled eggs mixed with melted butter and cooked polenta, scovergi – a version of cheese calzone, leek and black olive stew seasoned with garlic scapes, lovage garnished tomato soup, *mucenici* – a dessert served only on March 9, a Christian feast of the forty martyrs of Sebaste. Made of sweet dough and shaped like number eight, boiled in water with cinnamon and crushed nuts. They looked like edible garlands.

It took me six months to accept the idea that my son was going to my homeland, a place that didn't mean anything to him. A land that sounded exotic, intriguing in its resemblance to other former communist countries where people survived dictators that stripped them of humanity.

He called me every weekend. That became our weekly routine. Mother and son, drifting apart, but still connected.

I wrote to him every night for many months. I didn't leave my chair until two in the morning, my body melted into the wooden seat, my elbows resting on the table in an awkward position. All I wanted was to get out all these obsessive thoughts, the pain whose tentacles gripped my heart and wouldn't let go. I sat at my antique desk and wrote. I wrote until my hands were sore, my thumb and index finger clutched on the pen, my eyes blurry from crying, my head heavy with pain. I wrote to Matthew about my move to Canada, about the day when he was born, about the first steps that he took when he was eight months old, his first words, his first smile. I wanted to get everything out, a visceral feeling of giving birth, birthing a story, a story of love, and loneliness, and pain, and disappointment, a story that ached and healed at the same time.

I wrote him long letters, lamenting about his relocation choice, about Julia who had become excessive in her demands, spending all their money on daily trips to luxury malls. She quit her job at the British Council where she had been managing the Arts and Culture Department organizing events like the European Literature Night, British Documentary, and British Film Days. She didn't want to work in the pharmaceutical industry, but the fact that she had studied in Canada was an advantage, that's how she landed that job, which she so light-heartedly renounced.

"Matthew, why did Julia quit her job? I remember when I was a student in Bucharest, I dreamed about working there. What's wrong? Didn't she like it?" I asked him once.

The minute I asked these questions I realized I was accusing her, judging her, measuring her up to my own aspirations.

"Mom, that's none of your business. Why do you want to know?" Matthew's harsh voice screeched into my ear.

"I guess you're right, that's none of my business."

But I am your mom, I wanted to add, and my job is to worry, to take care of you, because you are my baby.

Matthew snapped at me: "Stop treating me like a baby."

After that conversation, I never asked him about Julia's pastimes or career choices. It was none of my business, right? I kept on with my life, but I sent him long letters although he laughed at me for not using email.

It felt like my heart would explode into tiny pieces, shooting through my throat, choking me.

"Mom, we shouldn't even have this conversation. I'm a grown man. I can make my own decisions. I know better. You keep nagging me just like you did with Dad."

"What do you know about your dad? You were four when we separated. I bet all you can remember are the presents he brought you every day."

"What's wrong with that, Mom? He wasn't a good dad?"

I was ashamed to admit I was wrong. With Matthew living in Romania, I felt that my life turned upside down again, just like it did after the divorce, when we sold the house and put everything in storage until we found a place.

One Saturday, a few weeks before my birthday, he told me about their trip to Horezu, a town known for its pottery.

"Mom, we bought hand-painted ceramics; it looks like Mexican Talavera pottery that we brought home from our vacation in Ixtapa. Remember?" Matthew said.

We had been to Mexico? Those were memories I had erased. But I did remember Horezu, a small town located three hours east of Bucharest, where the tradition of ceramic pottery had been kept alive for centuries. The craft had been passed on from one generation to another. Both women and men shaped the ceramic, with women decorating most of the pottery with the image of a rooster which was a symbol of the region.

It didn't surprise me that he discovered Romania through art.

"You know, Mom, I resented you for not letting me sign up for drama classes when I was in high school," he said. "I don't even remember how I ended up studying Chemistry."

"I don't know why I did it, Matthew. I wanted you to be tougher, to stand up for yourself, to not let anyone push you around."

"That's okay, Mom. I have no regrets. I really love my work. But life in Romania is not what I hoped it would be when I decided to move here with Julia. I can still see this lack of trust

146

that you told me about. It's endemic. Julia blames it on the many years of communism that encouraged people to spy on each other, to turn each other in for the slightest anti-government remarks. She sounds like you. I now understand why you left."

When he was a teenager, I kept lecturing him on how ungrateful he was, how he took everything for granted. He never listened. He knew better. He thought my unhealthy attachment to Canada was the result of my inability to come to terms with my departure.

"What did you expect? A country like Canada? Of course you're disappointed," I said.

Matthew continued as if he hadn't heard me.

"I look around and nothing seems familiar except for my life with Julia. Even that, at times, is bumpy and unpredictable like a long ride on the meandering roads outside Bucharest: a muddy countryside with patches of gravel marking the spots where some real estate moguls have built mansions in sheer contrast with the surrounding poverty".

What did I do to him? He started to sound just like me. On the other hand, his objective depiction of a society that used to be my home wasn't laden with discontent or pain. When I thought of painful events or places that inhabited my childhood, I felt trapped and liberated at the same time.

＊ ＊ ＊

After Matthew moved to Romania, I did a major purge.

"You have to let go," Katarina kept saying.

Let go? How could I let go? I didn't want to let go. Matthew was my love, my life, my everything, and his going away felt like a part of me turned into ashes. Gone. Forgotten.

Eventually I cleaned up his room, then the garage. I threw out all his schoolwork that I had kept in labelled boxes from grade one to grade twelve. Journal entries written diagonally in unintelligible cursive writing, stick people holding hands, A+ marked math worksheets, Pecha Kucha presentation slides, Mother's Day cards, diplomas, student of the month pins, and lots of scrunched up watercolors and abstract paintings that still smelled like him.

I sat down in his room and looked around. He had taken only a few clothes and books with him. Everything else was still there, as if it had been waiting for him to return. Basketball and soccer medals won only for showing up, framed jerseys, posters of his favourite players, a wooden Inukshuk that Keeran had brought from a short trip to Iqaluit, a blue dream catcher from Banff, friendship bracelets given by the few girls he liked when he was in high school, biology textbooks with paragraphs highlighted in green, dog-eared novels that he read and re-read until he knew them by heart: *All Quiet on the Western Front*, *One Hundred Years of Solitude*, *Beauty and Sadness*, *The Unbearable Lightness of Being*, *The Great Gatsby*, *The Naked and the Dead*, *The Alchemist*.

Each book that belonged to him brought back memories that I had forgotten. For Matthew, high school was a period of self-discovery and rebellion, not necessarily in that order. For me, it was a phase that I prayed would end without me losing my mind and him losing his way. I worked late almost every night, so Matthew was home alone after school. He joined a club that sounded like group therapy to me. A bunch of boys choking on their testosterone got together and talked about sports, the careers they wanted to pursue, and their immigrant parents who knew nothing about how the world worked. That was what I gathered from his attitude.

The longest conversations that we had during his excruciating four years of anticipated teenage freedom that gave him the right to yell 'leave-me-alone-you-don't-know-anything-I-hate-you-I-miss-Dad-you-have-no-idea-what-you're-talking-about-you-don't-make-any-sense-I-wish-you-were-not-my-Mom' were at the dinner table.

"Mom, I don't expect you to understand how I feel because you were not born here…and you're much older," he said.

"What does that have to do with anything? If you talk to me, I promise I'll listen. If you start with the assumption that I don't understand, then we're both wasting our time. The difference between you and me is that I've been your age. So, Mr. Know-It-All, tell me. What's on your mind?"

"Nothing."

"Nothing? Then why are you saying that I can't understand?"

"There's this girl at school… I like her."

My fourteen-year-old was in love. He thought he was in love. Just like that. Wasn't the boys' club supposed to be about boys' stuff? It looked like they talked about more than tournaments or how they could save the world. I promised I would listen, so I couldn't let him down. I re-organized the plates on the table, switched my cutlery from left to right, moved the water glass around my plate, wiped my mouth. I couldn't breathe. How I wished Keeran were there with us. He would have known how to deal with that. They would have had one of those "hey, man" conversations that women rarely understand.

"You see? What did I say? You don't get it."

"Honey, I didn't say anything. Now you're overreacting. I'm listening. I heard you. You like a girl. That's great! Do you want to talk about it?"

"No, I don't want to talk about it. You sound like your friend the therapist."

"My friend the therapist? You mean Katarina? Only your dad would say that."

"So what? What's so wrong about that?"

I had learned how to let go. Pretend I didn't hear. Show I didn't hurt.

That was the only time when I heard about his infatuation.

Almost as tall as his dad who, at six foot three, towered over everyone I knew, he looked more mature than I wanted him to be, but also more defiant. My ideas didn't make sense, our house wasn't big enough, my work wasn't as fascinating as his friends' parents' careers in research or luxury brands, my food was bland, I dressed like an old lady, and I bought way too many books that I never read.

"Dad said there's even a word for that: *tsundoku*. For people like you who keep piling up books that they never read. But I'm grateful for that, because I get to read them," he said.

Books offered us a reconciliation ground. Reading was the only passion that we shared. I did read most of the books I bought, but he was right. I acquired more than I could ever read. My obsession was easy to explain. At least, to myself. I grew up in a house without any fiction books. My parents rarely brought home any novels. Most of the books that they borrowed from the library or found at the local bookstore were language compendiums and history books dominated by communist interpretations of political events. Storytelling came in only one shape and colour: ideological indoctrination, the weapon of the political party that waved its red hammer and sickle flag over our lives.

Books gave me and Matthew an opportunity to talk. It was the only topic that helped me pull him closer even in moments when I was most afraid that he would drift away. Reading wasn't only a celebration of words or a storytelling feast, but it gave us a tacit understanding of each other's emotions. We knew, from what each of us was reading, if we felt distressed, happy, or apathetic.

"Mom, you're reading a memoir again. Did you have another argument with your boss?" he would say.

Memoirs were my go-to books when I felt discouraged. The grit, the perseverance, the resilience, the mental toughness that I found in those stories gave me the strength to move on. My drama was so inconsequential compared to what other people went through – torture, oppression, wars – that I felt like a dwarf apple tree in an apricot orchard.

Books also gave us a reason to fight. Over ideas, storylines, plots. It was a good fight. Matthew had a strong grasp of how to structure a story or build compelling characters, so in those instances roles were reversed – I was the disciple learning from the master.

He devoured all the shortlisted books for the Scotiabank Giller Prize – *The Time in Between* was his favourite – but he also enjoyed Harry Potter and *The Da Vinci Code*.

His love for books went beyond the required reading in school. He lost his interest in young adult fiction as soon as he discovered Gabriel García Márquez, Yasunari Kawabata, and Milan Kundera. Ever since he turned eleven, he enjoyed our weekly trips to the local library or Chapters Indigo where we sat on ottomans and read for hours, exchanging glances from time to time, and nodding at each other as if we had acquired some supernatural forces or a pearl of wisdom that allowed us to see into the future. He preferred to stay home and read instead of hanging out with his friends.

As I continued my purge, I found a few soccer jerseys and a pair of basketball shoes that he kept, I didn't know why. I kept the books and took everything else to The Salvation Army.

His room didn't look the same without all the knick-knacks that he had gathered over the years. The house didn't look the same. My life wasn't the same. I was like the last soldier standing on the barricade, fighting a battle that others had lost.

Solo un po'

California walnuts, sliced apples, dried figs, Muscat grapes, Parmigiano Reggiano, salt crackers, and a glass of Shiraz-Cabernet. That was the favourite appetizer Katarina and I always shared on my birthday. But not that year.

"Why parmesan cheese?" she asked me the first time I served her.

"I don't really know, but I remember watching this movie when I was a kid where a couple went to a restaurant and the server simply asked 'the usual?', to which they both nodded. They sat at the table for hours, talking and nibbling on the food, laughing, just being happy. Since then, a simple cheese platter with dry and fresh fruits puts me in a good mood."

Katarina found my preferences odd, like superstitions that one holds for comfort. I didn't disagree. Maybe she was right.

Before my forty-eighth birthday, she called me.

"No more cheese and crackers," she said. "I'll take you to a place that you'll simply love."

I trusted her instinct, so I accepted her invitation.

On the night of September 8, she came to my door, a bouquet of red roses in her hand.

"Come on, Ana. Let's go, let's go. You're gonna love it!" she said dragging me into a taxi.

It was a short ride to Lakeshore and Rosewood Avenue. We stopped in front of a newer building with offices on the top floor and stores and restaurants on the ground floor. On the side of the building, I could see the *trattoria* sign. Only Italians, known for their sartorial elegance and *pomodoro e basilico* dishes that epitomize sophistication in their simplicity, could call a restaurant *Solo un po'*. They could call it anything, because even the most prosaic name sounded romantic: Just a little. There was nothing *little* about the Italian greeter who hugged us as if we had been his long-time friends. With large gestures, he showed us to our table confirming our names in a loud voice.

"Signorina Lhotzky and Owen. *Da questa parte, per favore.*"

Clearing the air in front of us with grand hand movements, he pulled two chairs and waited for us to sit down before placing the menus on the dark wood table.

The subdued elegance of the minimalist décor reminded me of airport lounges – half-corporate, half-casual. Turquoise walls bordered by camel baseboards contrasted with the dark furniture and sage green silk linen placemats.

Navigating the Italian menu felt like an unplanned quiz given by a waiter who saw himself more like an educator willing to share his knowledge and test ours. *Pane carasau, calamari alla griglia,* risotto-style fregula with mushrooms, abbamele and goat cheese, *cavatelli al sugo d'agnello*. I understood only a couple of words that sounded like food. I didn't pass the test, so I asked for the daily special.

During dinner, Katarina was suspiciously quiet. She answered all my questions in monosyllabic words that, despite her efforts to look present, didn't mean anything.

"Katarina, what's wrong? You keep shutting me down. You are the one who invited me here, remember? Besides, you are the storyteller, the therapist, the talker. What happened? Do you want to go?"

"Nope."

It was late into the night when we finished our meal with *dulce de leche panna cotta* and espresso, and when Katarina finally started talking.

"Ana, do you remember when we met for the first time? At that Italian restaurant in North York? I'm sure you do, but that's not the point. For over ten years, you have been part of my life. I lived, and laughed, and cried, and suffered, and dreamed, and hoped with you. For you. You are the sister that I've never had. Anyway, I just wanted to say that you are my everything. Oh, God, that sounds so clichéd."

I just sat there, looking at her, imagining how our lives might change. Two women sharing a past, not sure about the future. I imagined how every year after that we would celebrate my birthday at *Solo un po'*. A name that held the promise of a little happiness, *un po 'di felicità*.

Just a little happiness. That's what I was looking for when I came to Canada, and it bothered me when people kept asking dumb questions about me.

"You look preoccupied," said Katarina.

"It's nothing. I just remembered this. Random thought. I know people are just trying to be nice, but can they, please, stop mistaking Bucharest for Budapest? We're talking about two different countries: Romania and Hungary! I don't know, it just bothers me when people try so hard to make small talk and they cannot even locate these two countries on the map."

Katarina tried to calm me down.

"Why are you so worked up, anyway?"

"Of course, they want to ask all these questions, as if they were truly interested in hearing the answer. So how are things in Romania now? Have they changed since the collapse of communism?"

I don't know, I feel like yelling in their face, and I don't fucking care because I don't live there anymore.

"Every time, I keep my composure and answer politely, recounting the latest BBC or CNN news I've read online. Just like any other Canadian who has no interest in sensational live news about a country where dozens of stray dogs litter the streets, scandals about corrupt politicians erupt every day, and young girls no longer dream of being the next Nadia Comăneci but instead aspire to become some local celebrity who drives a Ferrari and can't tell Toronto from Torino."

"Now you sound crazy. Did this happen recently? You remind me of my clients."

Katarina lived for her clients. Messed up couples, alcoholic divorcés, confused teenagers, postpartum depressed mothers; they all came to her like honeybees attracted to wildflowers. It was easy for them to talk to her.

"How's Matthew doing? Does he still like it in Romania? When was the last time you spoke with him?"

That's how Katarina was, asking three questions at the same time, not giving you enough time to respond. I hesitated, because I didn't want her to know that I missed him so much. Although he was in his early twenties, he was still my baby.

"He's fine. He enjoys his job, you know. Goes out a lot with his co-workers. Likes exploring the historic downtown."

"Ana, take me to Romania one day. Why don't we go there together for Christmas? Can we get any good flight deals? Would we have a place to stay, or would we need to book a hotel?"

"Katarina, you need to focus more. You keep asking so many questions, I don't even have time to respond. But you know what? That's not a bad idea. The only downside is that the city gets too slushy when the weather is bad, almost non-walkable. But let's look up flight options. I would love to go back and visit."

"Is Matthew renting or is he staying at Julia's house? By the way, do you remember when you refused to buy Matthew a proper desk chair because you didn't want him to get too comfortable when he was doing his homework?"

Where did this come from?

"He's staying with Julia, and yes, I do," I admitted right away. I could not believe I did that to my own son; forcing him to sit in a chair for hours on end solving math problems, looking up words in an online dictionary, drawing, writing. That was exactly what my parents had done to me. I didn't elaborate on this story with Katarina who had a gift of making me feel guilty for the slightest failure that I felt as a mother. She was my best friend but at times she knew how to unveil this crudeness in me that made me ashamed.

"Do you remember when you made mushroom risotto?"

"Of course, I did. Not as good as the food here, but not bad either. You brought wine."

Katarina loved red wine. A self-entitled connoisseur who developed her taste through travelling, tasting, and experimenting, she first checked out my improvised wine cellar consisting of a small wooden rack stowed away in a basement closet, then came upstairs and took a bottle of wine out of her purse.

It was a bottle of Dornfelder, a fragranced, fruity German wine that was one of her favourites. She was a vast encyclopedia when it came to German wines. I wasn't sure if that was because she really liked the wine or she liked it because it was German, and it reminded her of her own roots. Although white wine wasn't on her preferred list, she knew all the grape varieties by heart – Grauburgunder, Kerner, Müller-Thurgau, Scheurube, Weissburgunder. The reds and sweet wines always made her list. That was how I learned that over half of German wines were dry or medium-dry and their dessert wines resembling the Canadian ice wine were quite sensational.

"I won't argue with you. You are the connoisseur."

I remembered how we sat down at the dinner table and, as I watched Katarina pouring the wine in the Riedel glasses purchased from Home Sense the day before, I thought, 'What a perfect moment!' Just like the one we were having. *Un po 'di felicità.*

* * *

"Ana, what's your secret nationality?" Katarina said during one of our walks in Port Credit.

"Hum? Secret nationality?" I said.

"Yes. Most immigrants like my parents and you have a secret nationality. Not defined by cultural boundaries or confined to a certain land. The feeling of displacement that you have and maybe continue to experience didn't start in Canada, but back in your country. That's why you felt the urge to leave," she said.

"That's an interesting theory. Ha, ha, ha, did you make it up?" I said.

"No, I didn't. Okay, it may sound stereotypical, but it's based on the idea that each country has its own characteristics shared by its people. Let's take Germany, for example. Everyone

I know believes Germans are obsessed with quality, are nationalistic, and have a work ethic that no one can match. Also, they live with this permanent guilt of producing a monstrous leader who orchestrated the death of millions of Jews."

"That sounds about right," I said.

"You see, even you are biased. Everyone is. We can also agree that we base our opinions on historical truths or statements that are backed by statistical data – think of German cars. But my parents are not like that. My relatives are not, either. Don't tell me they are just exceptions. So, there's a questionnaire that you can do. Based on your response, you find out your secret nationality. My parents' is Italian. Who would have thought? Mine is Spanish. I bet yours is Spanish, too," she said.

"Okay, that sounds like a bunch of crap. Where did you find this questionnaire? Let me do it and I'll prove you wrong."

Katarina grabbed my elbow. We walked in silence for another half an hour.

When I got home that night, I kept thinking about what she said. If everyone had a secret nationality, then would that dictate our destiny at birth? I wished I believed in the three Moirai determining my destiny by stumbling upon Canada. Or just Clotho spinning the thread of my life onto her spindle by tracing a path on a globe that she spun with her eyes closed. Let me place my finger at random and see where it stops. Where did I land? Canada, eh? Good enough.

Or maybe it was a secret spell my parents cast on me during the baptism ceremony when the Orthodox priest chanted his words while sealing me with chrism after the threefold immersion in water. A spell they would never divulge or undo. A pact that they made to let me choose my nationality when I grew up.

Later that night, Katarina sent me the online quiz that took five minutes to complete. Where else in the world could I find people who were like me? After I answered a few questions that measured my openness, conscientiousness, and agreeableness, I discovered that my personality would feel best at home in… France. The second time I did it, I turned out to be Bangladeshi. Hoping the third would be the luckiest, I tried again. Finnish.

Whether my secret nationality was Bangladeshi, Canadian, French, Romanian, or Finnish, it didn't matter. What mattered was that I chose to live in a country that slowly felt like my true home.

Craving sameness

I sat at my desk trying to fool myself into writing in the silence of the night, interrupted by the whirring and zooming of the old dishwasher whose rust stains I had fixed up with a black permanent marker. What was Katarina doing? How was she feeling? What new foods was she eating? What did I want to say to her, in response to her unexpected email that I had received the day before?

From: klhotzky@yahoo.ca
Subject line: Hello from India
Sent on: Saturday, October 19, 2013

Hi there,

I know you're mad at me because I simply disappeared, and I didn't even warn you. That I didn't tell anyone. After we had that nice dinner – I loved the pane carasau – I went home, packed up my stuff, gave the keys to my neighbour Aramis, I jumped in a cab and off I went. Do you remember him? The guy who always mowed my lawn when he did his. A nice guy, "ein netter Kerl", as my parents liked to say, hoping the two of us would hook up, but they didn't know he had a partner ☺.

I lied to you, Ana. I'm not the strong woman I've tried so hard to pose as all these years. I'm just as fragile, messed up, and disoriented as all my clients. I couldn't take it anymore. All the sessions where I sat and listened to these stories of people drowning, suffocating in their own lives, all the bullshit about cognitive behavioural therapy, all the listening, the nodding, the pretense, the hiding, I just couldn't. As a counsellor, I always told my clients to let it out. Talk or write about it. Start with words that you like. Words that you loathe. Words that haunt you. Words that soothe you. Words that keep you up at night. Like sinuous stories that startle you in your sleep, waking you up, only to realize that these are not just the product of your imagination. They are memories buried deep into your subconscious that you pushed, and pushed, and pushed, and never let them come to the surface until an event, a smell, a conversation, an encounter, a landscape, or a person forces them out, like a pump valve explosion when the water stream shoots out.

It's the kind of memories that drag you down, abysmal emotions dripping like vinegar into an open wound. You tap, tap, tap, but it keeps dripping; the pain is so intense, that your sense of time and space fades into an indefinite dimension of your existence.

I had to decide, to find a way out. I'm missing you so much, but I knew this would happen the minute I stepped out of the house, one small suitcase in my right hand, and the Lacoste purse that you gave me in the other (do you remember the gift card that you got from a friend of yours and you waited for three years until you gave it to me? You're a re-gifter, my darling). Almost sleepwalking, I got on a flight to London, and from there to India, where I went to an Ashram. I wanted to get a hug from this guru whom everyone

162

considers a saint. Amma. Have you heard of her? Do you know her story? A friend of mine who lives in Prague waited in line for five hours to get a hug. The way she described it was beyond my understanding. She felt this huge weight taken off her chest instantly. I found it hard to believe.

As a therapist, I seek scientific methods to help my clients. Although I tried meditation once, many years ago, I don't consider myself a very spiritual person. The way she described her experience tells me something might be out there, just waiting for me to discover it.

Now, I've been here for a couple of weeks, trying to settle in, practising silence and meditation. I've been told she travels a lot, but she comes here quite often, so I can't wait to meet her. There's nothing esoteric about this experience, I just want to meet this amazing woman who dedicates her life to spreading the message that the lack of love leads to pain and disharmony in this world. Wouldn't that be sweet? That, instead of prescribing antidepressants to my clients, their family doctors would send them off to find some love in their life? Or even better, have a 'love pill' like an over-the-counter drug. 'Ms. So-and-So, what would you prefer? Antidepressants or the love pill?'

I must go now. I need to practice my silence ☺.

I know we talked about going to Romania together when we met last time. I'd really love to go with you there one day. Please be patient with me.

If you decide to go by yourself, please say 'Hi' to Matthew. I miss you.

Katarina

I read her email over and over again. How could she do this to me? I needed her. She helped me regain my balance and then she left. Gone. I had known Katarina for so many years, that she had become part of my life, she had become a part of me. After the divorce, I told her about this guy I had met at work, Karl, whose name tickled her ears.

"Aha, a German guy. Now, we're talking, *meine liebe*!" she said triumphantly.

"Why are you so happy?" I asked. "He's not my boyfriend. It's nothing, really."

"I know, Ana. I'm just saying…"

I didn't mind the fact she was taking so much interest in my love life. I know she wanted me to be happy, but sometimes I couldn't figure her out. It almost felt like I was her project, her pet. After getting over the anger caused by her departure, I decided to reply. After all, didn't she teach me I had to be kinder to people, because everyone fought a hard battle?

From: aowen55@hotmail.com
Subject line: Wie geht's dir?

Hallo Katarina,

Wie geht's dir? ☺ *You see, I'm practising the German that you taught me.*

I'm quite mad that you left without telling me, but I understand. From all the people you know, aren't you surprised that I'm the one who understands this crazy decision of yours to fly to India, a country that you despised for its contrasts, crowds, and slums? I sit at the dinner table by myself, recalling the last meal I shared with you. The food doesn't taste the same. When will you come back? Why did you go there? Did you make any new friends?

See you soon! Wir sehen uns bald
Ana

I didn't tell her I used an online dictionary, as she was a traditionalist when it came to learning a foreign language; she had me do it the old way, with a pencil, a grammar book, and a notepad on my side.

Her going away left a hole in my heart. I couldn't find my place anymore. I looked forward to her emails. I woke up in the middle of the night, trying to figure out if she was ten hours ahead or behind. No, Romania was seven hours ahead, and India was …wait a minute, was it behind? No, dammit, it was ahead. Why did I find it so hard to remember?

Her messages were coming as precise as an authentic German clock. Every Friday morning, I had my coffee at eight o'clock, surfed the net, browsed the top stories on CNN, BBC, and CBC websites, killing time until eight-thirty when I would log into my Hotmail account. I became dependent on the bold font in my inbox.

I set up my email to preview all the messages before I opened them. To keep the illusion of surprise. Hers I opened right away.

I wondered why she left without saying good-bye. I remembered how, in the weeks before her sudden departure, she philosophized on topics that touched my life in so many ways. Above all, I relived our long conversations about why she believed I had changed.

"You need to stop trying to create this optimal version of yourself, envisioning one single path that will bring you to a perfectly happy life, because there's no such a thing."

As I reminisced about our talks, her words echoed in my mind as a monologue that I wasn't supposed to hear.

"We spend our youth trying to prove ourselves, wasting time with social comparisons, trying to be someone else, wishing to wake up one day and transform not into an insect, but into a flower. Exotic, unique, coveted. We try so hard to impress, to live up to someone else's standards, that we forget to live our lives. We forget that who we are is more important than what others want us to be or appear," she said. "Even you, look at you. When you came to Canada you wanted so much to belong that you kept hiding what made you different. You craved the sameness as hard as pregnant women crave food. Don't look at me that way, I'm just like you. I'm an educated woman working toward an ideal of myself that even I find difficult to define. Marriage and divorce changed your perspective. Anyone can see that. You are 'the belligerent immigrant who turned indifferent'," she said. "Ana, what switch in your mind did you turn on or off? What happened to the angry woman that I met upon her arrival in Canada? I never thought you would stop worrying about other people's opinions of you, how they see you," she said.

"They don't. They don't see me for who I am, they see me only in connection with Keeran. I was his wife. Nothing more. Even his parents looked through me when they talked to me," I said.

She was right. I didn't care. Because I didn't need to prove anything to anyone. Gone were the days when I pondered over my decision to come to a country where I knew no one. And the moments when I thought I would never learn how to navigate this system.

"Still, something happened. I need to understand what and why," Katarina said.

"Take your therapist's hat off and leave me alone. I don't need to explain anything. Weren't you the one who said you knew everything about me? Well, this is your chance to prove it," I said.

"I do, I do. I do know everything about you, but this is such a dramatic change that I can't fathom Ana's conversations not being imbued with anger and frustration," she said.

"Well, get used to it. Get used to the new Ana. Wiser, calmer, happier," I said.

"That's easy, but boring. I don't need boring friends. I've got lots of those. Or used to rather. Predictable, compliant, safe. What I liked most about you was that restlessness, that…I don't know…how should I describe it, the discontent that came from your fearlessness. Who is this mellow woman willing to give up a good fight in the name of inner peace? I don't recognize her," she said.

"Katarina, I have no idea what you're talking about. I'm the least fearless person I know. That was me as much as this is me. Did all these years of treating people with all sorts of issues get you used to drama-filled lives that need to be fixed? I don't need any fixing. I'm fine," I said.

"You got me all wrong. That's not what I meant. You know how much I love you. Don't let this experience change you. That's all I'm saying. I mean, let it change you, but don't let it define you," she said.

I didn't realize until that night that Katarina was as broken as her own patients. My drama mattered, but what about hers? We both shared the right to tell our stories.

"Tell me. Are you ever jealous of your patients who over-come hurdles and save their relationships?" I said.

"Oh, fuff, now you think you're the therapist. Mwah!" she said, blowing me a kiss.

"No, seriously. I'm curious. Please be honest," I said.

"Okay, okay, I'll be honest. I just like teasing you. I must admit, off the record, that sometimes I feel this urge to tell them, especially women, 'Don't go back. That's not the right man for you.' Not because I'm jealous, but because in more than fifty percent of cases, they end up in a divorce. It's a pattern that I've seen emerging in that type of dynamic. Fights, anger, zero libido, affairs, make-up sex, and then emptiness. Sheer emptiness," she said, touching my hand.

We were sitting on a Starbucks patio on Lakeshore and Front Street in Port Credit. The early November weather kept most customers inside. Two couples in their late twenties were flanking our table, taking a furtive look at us as I pulled my hand away. Shortly after, a light drizzle covered the patio stones in a layer of glossy beads like illuminator drops on a woman's cheekbones. That place was one of our usual spots where we met after Katarina finished her sessions of "fixing broken people."

Pretzels for New Year's Eve

How could I accept that Matthew was a grown-up in charge of his own life, able to make his own decisions without consulting with me? Keeran tried to stay in the picture by calling me every few months to ask about him and his life in Romania.

"You know you can call him in Bucharest, right? I gave you his phone number."

"Why would I do that? He made it clear he didn't want me in his life," Keeran said.

He did? I tried to remember how or when that happened, but the only interaction between them that touched on this topic didn't have the ultimatum that he implied.

"Well, I don't know how you got that impression. It's your choice."

"MY choice? What do you mean? It was his choice to move. I will never go there to visit him. Why would I? What's there to see anyway? Not to mention your parents. Jeez, what kind of family are you coming from? I told Devin about them. I wonder if dementia runs in your family."

"Keeran, why did you call exactly? To lash out at us? What do you want? I can talk with you if you have a valid argument. So far, you've been criticizing everyone in my family, in your family, as a matter of fact. It's rather late for you to assume the role of the caring father."

"Whatever, I can never talk to you. You get so defensive. In your mind, everything I say is a personal attack. Tell Matthew I've called when you speak with him," he said hanging up.

Farewells were not his forte. Nor was diplomacy. Why did he get a second chance at life? I didn't. Why was he in a happy relationship? I wasn't.

I was defensive? Of course, I was. All he cared about was to remind us he was the only one who was always right. Mr. Right, just like his mom. Perfect in their choices, polished in their opinions, ambitious in their desires. I was unfit. Always on guard. Never taken seriously. Matthew didn't want to hear about these calls, so I didn't share too much with him. I didn't have a compelling enough reason to persuade him to get in touch with his dad, but I believed in the universality of basic emotions, so I trusted Matthew would eventually suppress his anger, and start loving or at least respecting Keeran again. Other than the calls when I was slammed for failing to guide Matthew onto the right path and for doing zippo to dissuade him from following his girlfriend to a country that meant nothing to him, he rarely called. I didn't bother to ask too many questions about his newly found happiness.

As time went by, his calls were less bitter, his tone softened, but still disapproving.

"I still don't understand. Why does he want to live there? The proximity of other countries is appealing, I get it. He can drive to Vienna or Prague for a long weekend. He can fly anywhere in Europe in a matter of hours. At affordable prices, not like in Canada. But still. The corruption, the culture. Everything is so different. Does he even speak Romanian at the level required for his job?"

"He speaks English at work. His Romanian is decent, he can get by."

Curt replies worked best during those conversations. When punctuated with meh and eh, my sentences didn't elicit too much negative response from him. Our calls always ended on an ambiguous note that made me believe I shouldn't expect another one soon.

* * *

A couple of days after Christmas, I received another call in the middle of the night.

"Ana, we're at the hospital. You must come home. Your mom had a stroke, that's what the neurologist said," I heard him whispering on the phone as if he didn't really want to be heard.

What did he want me to do? Jump on the plane and fly to Romania? As if my life didn't matter, as if I didn't have anything better to do. Why wasn't he taking care of her? Wasn't that what husbands and wives were supposed to do? Now he remembered he had a family. That his daughter was the one who always dropped everything and ran to his side when he needed help.

"I don't understand. What are you saying? How did this happen? She was in good health. How is this possible? I bet you fed her those homemade sausages of yours."

I couldn't believe I said that, as if my mom were a baby who needed to be fed, who couldn't make her own choices.

"Listen, Dad, I'm sorry," I heard myself saying.

"That's okay, Ana. I'm used to your reproachful tone. And, no, I didn't feed her any sausages. This is not something recent. It's a problem that's been going on for years. Her carotid artery got blocked. This is not something that happened overnight."

I booked my flight right away. A blizzard stormed through Toronto, which caused massive delays at Pearson Airport, where thousands of passengers crammed into uncomfortable seats by the gates were waiting impatiently.

Someone next to me had left a glossy magazine on the chair. The front cover featured a glamorous loft with floor to ceiling windows that reflected the CN Tower in the distance. It must have been a real estate agent or a buyer looking for the perfect living space in one of those old factories turned into sought-after buildings promising a lifestyle worthy of rising Hollywood celebrities. I should have moved into one of those downtown places instead of living in the suburbs.

In front of me, a couple in their late fifties or early sixties were sitting with their hands crossed over their knees. They looked like two parents teleported from the Romanian countryside, ending their visit with their Canadianized children. The woman wore a traditional Romanian blouse, intricately stitched on the sleeves, with bright red embroidery on the chest – two oversized poppies with parakeet green stems running down to the hem. The man's handwoven silver-blue belt matched his wife's blouse through the embroidery that showed the hand of an artisan.

I wished my parents had been like that. Proudly wearing authentic clothing that would have made them easily identifiable as Romanian. Their patriotism, though, was limited to singing the national anthem during sports events that they sometimes watched on TV. Their sense of national identity or

172

association with traditional values was too vague for me to articulate. We were two lost generations – one buried in the sordidness of communism, the other adrift in a new democracy that failed to inspire.

I continued to scan the crowd of passengers, waiting patiently to board the plane. A young family to my left rummaged through their carry-on and produced colouring books and crayons for their twin toddler boys.

Dressed in ripped jeans and a gray sweatshirt, the man looked like a teenager. Most likely, a software developer for a financial institution, spending his days on Bay Street, commuting from a suburb east of Toronto, maybe Whitby or Ajax. The woman must have been a teacher, judging by how she transformed the *I Spy* book into classroom material.

"Tristan, let's look at this page together. Can you, please, focus? How many rings can you find?"

"I spy with my little eye… Mommy, I can see one ring, look," the boy said.

"Look again, I said you need to focus, why don't you focus?" the mom said.

"Okay, mommy. I spy with my little eye… er, mommy, one," the boy said.

"That's right. So, one plus one equals…?" she asked loudly as if she were showcasing her son's mental abilities in front of a junior kindergarten examination committee.

I looked around me trying to find sadness on people's faces. Who were all those passengers who packed up their bags and decided to fly on New Year's Eve? Why were they travelling on a night when you were supposed to stay with friends and family and party through the late hours? A night when you shared your New Year's resolutions, proclaiming that the following year you would keep your promises, you would lose those extra pounds, you would read more, you would carve in more time for yourself, you would be kinder, more generous, more open-minded.

My New Year's dinner was a bag of mini pretzels, coleslaw, vegetarian pasta, and a chocolate brownie. When the clock struck midnight, I sipped my red wine from a paper cup listening to the crew captain who briefly interrupted the British Airways news to wish us Happy New Year.

Under normal circumstances, spending New Year's Eve over the Atlantic Ocean would have been quite romantic. I looked around and I saw people hugging, cheering, laughing, smiling, talking. Healthy people who were able to share their thoughts, to communicate so easily. I imagined my mom lying in a hospital bed in Romania and I pictured her holding out her hands like an actress in a silent movie. Her lips were moving, but no sounds came out. Her communication was now limited to smiles and gentle hand strokes, reminding me of an old cartographer tracing lines on an ancient map, in an effort to revive a lost world.

She had an ischemic stroke. That's what the doctor said. Fatty deposits that had built up in her carotid artery over the years stopped the blood flow to her brain. Despite a speedy response from emergency services, she had remained half-paralyzed and lost her speech.

The stroke had also severed the invisible connection with my dad, after fifty years of marriage. Like tourists stranded on a foreign land, they discovered a new language, the language of touch and short sentences, of unspoken words. The speech therapist wasn't optimistic about her recovery and, given the limited resources available at the University Hospital in Bucharest, I knew those sessions wouldn't last long.

After her release from the hospital, my parents learned how to live a life without words. I joined my dad in his efforts to decipher a cryptic smile, interpret an unusual sound, or decode a fleeting touch. I trained myself to believe that, in my mom's mind, each gesture, every smile, any movement had their own meaning that words could no longer describe.

If I were to pick a moment in my life when everything changed, what would that be? Would that be the day when I chose which high school to go to? The university that took me away from my parents? Would that be the moment when I became a mother, when I knew my life would never be the same? Or was it the day when my mom had a stroke and in a matter of minutes she transformed from a healthy and beautiful, though forgetful, woman into a frail sick patient who depended on others to change her diaper, bring her food, or sponge wash her body?

For six months, I hoped she would eventually talk to me again, her limp arm would rest on my hand when I sat on the side of her bed. I hoped she would come out of darkness and tell me a story so I could understand why it happened.

It felt like she was dying a slow death. Not like the kind of death that cancer brought, but a different kind that made everyone else feel guilty. A guilt that made us fit her memories into our daily life, bringing up her name in conversations unrelated to her, displaying her photographs on shelves meant not for obituaries, but for celebrating life.

"Dad, I have to go back. I can't stay with you."

"Of course you can't. Why would you? You have your own life, right?"

"Yes, Dad, I do have my own life. I promise I'll call you."

He didn't talk to me until I left.

"Call me, Ana. Call me."

Wounded soldier

From: klhotzky@yahoo.ca
Subject line: Braun Büffel Purse
Sent on: Wednesday, January 15, 2014

Hi Ana,

I know you look forward to these emails as much as I do. It's really flattering to know there is at least one person in this world who looks up to me, who feels my absence as a hard rock chained to her ankles, dragging her down; someone who misses me unconditionally.

You know, I'm not really the nice, thorough, and balanced person you believe I am. Well, I'm not. I've tried all my life to be all these things and I failed miserably. I tried because others depended on me, or that's what I thought, and I couldn't let them down. I got this from my dad. He was like that. His health was bad, his finances were low, but he never said 'No' to a friend who needed his help, neglecting me and my mom because, in his view, family didn't need reassurance. We were always there.

Now I did exactly what my dad did all the time. It's not that you are my family, but you are as close as I can get to someone.

Hey, do you remember the Braun Büffel bag you liked so much? I left it at my mom's. Please go and pick it up when you have time. Do you still have those chocolate brown suede shoes you bought in Barcelona when you went on vacation with your cousin Tudor? They're a perfect match.

I'm rambling about my problems, and I didn't tell you anything about this place. I'm still waiting for this acclaimed woman to arrive. You know I'm not a spiritual person and, despite my parents' efforts to teach me strong Catholic values, I have never been the obedient child ready to follow orders or say my prayers before every meal. I got to a point in my life when I had to try and find a higher meaning. I know it may sound phony coming from me, but I'm dead serious. I want to be able to come back, do my job. I still want to believe I'm part of something special, a profession that allows me to peek into people's hearts, take out their fears, shake them up, bandage them like wounded soldiers, and send them back into the battle. Has anyone ever won a war without wounded soldiers?

I will stay here until I see this guru. Yes, that's what I want to do.

Are you still going to Erindale Park? I miss those long walks with you. When my mom asked me what we talked about all that time, I said 'nothing'. 'What do you mean, nothing? You just walk side by side and say nothing?' She couldn't believe it. 'Yes, Mom, we don't need to speak. It's walking in silence, something that we learned how to do together. It's relaxing. You should try it'.

I know you're curious to find out what it's like here. This is my little retreat. I don't want to share it with anyone; I hope you understand.

Anyway, I must go. I met this young woman from Germany who insists on speaking German to me, and I cannot resist it ☺

PS – Did you find someone else who has a special place in your heart?

I turned off my laptop and got ready to go to work. Another day in a place where young colleagues complained they were trapped in unfulfilling jobs, where people close to retirement refused to use voicemail or email, a place where I felt like a bridge between the nit-picking millennials and the blasé baby boomers. As annoying as those young people were, at least Justin was gracious enough to give me my job back.

That night, I went for a long walk in Erindale Park, one of my favourite places in Mississauga. I enjoyed the winding road by Credit River. It was a nice hike, unlike other places where the path was going in circles around the park, forcing me to pass the same trees, see the same people, hear the same sounds. I liked the swish of the river frothing up when it hit the big rocks, swirling like a whirlpool. It was one of the quiet walks that I liked to take before I made a big decision. In a way, it calmed me down, but it also stirred something up in me, something that gave me the courage to do things that I was afraid of.

I went back to an empty house and made myself a quinoa salad with slivered almonds, dry cranberries, flaxseed, and feta cheese. Most of my life I had been a soup eater, but, after Katarina had left, I developed an unusual preference for salads, some of them quite exotic that I surprised myself by mixing in pomegranate seeds, mango slices, or red grapes.

In the evening, I called Katarina's mom.

"Hi, Mrs. Lhotzky, it's Ana."

"Ana. I can't believe that after so many years you still call me Mrs. Lhotzky. How are things?" she said. Her calming voice reminded me of my first encounter with Katarina. It had the same low soothing pitch that won me over.

"Not bad, not bad. Hm, Katarina sent me an email, she said I should come by and pick up a purse that she left for me."

"Oh, yes, she called me the other day".

She called her? How come she never called me?

"Can I come now?"

"What time will you get here?"

"Half an hour."

"Okay, see you then."

I drove to Port Credit where Mrs. Lhotzky had an old house facing the ravine. When I met Katarina, they had a pool in the backyard, but by the time she moved out, they decided to close it down.

"Are you, guys, closing it down for the winter?" I remember asking her.

"No, silly, we're going to remove it. Dad says it's not worth it, too much work for the little time that we get to enjoy it during the summer."

It took me about twenty minutes to get there. No sooner had I rung the bell than Mrs. Lhotzky opened the door for me.

"Hi, Ana, please come in," she said and hugged me before I could say anything.

Her house smelled of lavender and vanilla, a heavy fragrance that gave me headaches. I remembered once, when her parents were out, Katarina and I took all the diffusers, the candles, the perfumed gel beads, and the potpourri. We put them away in a basement cabinet and took them out only a few minutes before her parents came back. Now the intense fragrance almost choked me. My breathing slowed down, my head pressure tightened up as if it was clutched between a plate and flywheel causing me vertigo.

"Do you mind if I won't come in? I cannot stay, I'm working on this new project, and I need to finish something up tonight, my boss needs it first thing tomorrow morning."

"On Saturday? Oh, my goodness, what has this world come to? When I was your age, such demands would have been unimaginable," I heard her say as she was huffing up the stairs. She returned with the purse. I loved that colour.

"Is this the one?"

"Yes, that's the one. Thank you, Mrs. Lhotzky. I promise I'll call again and next time I'll stay longer."

I closed the door behind me, rushed to the car and, before I turned the ignition on, I opened the purse where I found a silver-gray Estée Lauder cosmetics bag with lipsticks, eye shadow, and mascara. I took out the lipsticks, opened them one by one, smelled them, and put them back. Katarina was the one who talked me into trying on the weirdest shades that reminded me of chocolate, frozen grapes, and Starbucks: Crazy for Coffee, Summer Sunset, Almost Blushing, Pure Plum, Caramel Macchiato, Hazelnut Cappuccino, Neige Blanche, Iced Peppermint Mocha.

Procustean bed

Katarina sporadically emailed me until she stopped completely. The last message I received in my inbox was dated February 14, 2014.

"In stark contrast to the life I lead, governed by my patients' stories and my own interpretation of their conundrums, the silence that surrounds me here is apocalyptic. At first, I saw it as a blessing, but slowly I've come to realize it invites only abysmal thoughts. Wasn't this supposed to have healing powers? All I can think of every day as I take in the mountain view is that soon I will find myself a lonely old woman forgotten in a suburban house in a neighbourhood where the only sound that gives away the existence of life is the puck hit by twelve-year-old boys playing street hockey. My days would be as endless and intolerable as the horizon, punctuated by the Canada Post delivery guy knocking on my door to warn me that my mailbox is chuck full of unsolicited flyers yet again. I would reluctantly have coffee and toast in the morning, like a mental health patient forced to take her pills, beet salad for lunch, and fish fingers for supper, most of my meals delivered by truck every day. I would turn on the TV now and then, hoping for a show rerun or some music videos from the 80s, leafing through old magazines that I have

subscribed to before retirement - 'APS Observer', 'Psychological Bulletin', 'The Psychologist'. Every Sunday, I would clean up the fridge, purging any unfinished meals stowed away in white and blue containers. I would go for a stroll, exchanging a few pleasantries with dog owners whose brisk walk would make me dizzy, and return home with a few silky chestnuts or a couple of forsythia sprigs, depending on the season.

My laptop and phone would be turned off, severing my only connection with the people I know.

At night, I would fall asleep between two king size pillows, and dream of unfinished projects or places that I didn't get to see. I would wake up every three hours just to check the time on the antique alarm clock whose golden hands would shine in the dark and remind me I was still alive.

I won't have a child or a friend to check up on me. I would think of all the patients whom I hoped I had helped and continue to doubt whether the long conversations muffled between the soundproof walls of my office had the outcome they deserved.

You've asked me many times why I chose this career, and I never told you the truth. When I was in high school, my best friend committed suicide. Out of the blue. Her name was Isabella. Isabella Martinez Flores. Born on the same day as I. We were like sisters. Both single children, we became friends in grade six and, from then onwards, we were inseparable. Same class, same summer camps, many sleepovers, and, later, school dances and double dates. Our dream was to marry two brothers and share a big house by the ocean. Prince Edward Island or Saint Pierre and Miquelon. We would both be teachers. Have a large family and live together happily thereafter. In grade eleven, she fell in love with this guy who was, according to many, the most popular athlete in our school: good at all sports, liked by all girls, favoured by male teachers, but not excelling at anything else. His weak academic results won him the 'Strong, but Wrong' nickname. Every answer he gave in class was off-topic, followed by thumbs-up chants from his cheerleaders. After going on a few dates with him, she stopped coming to my house. Every time I called, she was busy or out with him. In only a few months, she transformed into one of the many girls who hung out with muscle shirts at the mall and smoked pot in the school bathroom.

'Katarina, you're so preoccupied with your studies, that you don't even realize what you're missing out on. Girls our age have fun. Do you even know what that is? You're gonna die a virgin, I'm telling you. You have no idea. I love you, but I don't want to end up like you,' I remember her saying the last night I saw her.

She was on her way to one of the many parties that she went to with her Strong, but Wrong boyfriend. He was supposed to come and pick her up, but one hour before their date, he called to let her know he couldn't make it. She had to drive herself. He would see her at the party. I found out the details from her parents. She was upset when she left the house. She had cried in her room until the smudged mascara under her eyes made her look like a raccoon. She never reached the party. The police report showed she had driven over the concrete wall flying over Highway 401 at the spaghetti junction at Highway 427. She was killed on impact. That was what the police said. She didn't suffer. She died instantly. Her mother was the one who answered the phone when the constable called.

By the time I finished high school, everyone had forgotten about Isabella. I couldn't share my memories about her with anyone else. Only her parents, whom I called once after the funeral which the entire class had attended.

As much as I tried, I could no longer make any friends. All the people I met were only shoddy substitutes for Isabella who, somehow, became the Procustean bed of my relationships. It was like a curse that I carried into my practice - judging my patients by an imaginary standard that even I failed to meet. I felt guilty for all the troubled teenagers who divulged their darkest secrets in front of me - they left my office more adrift, less certain, more doubtful. Now and then, I would get a call from their parents to let me know that they no longer required my service. How did those kids, surrounded by so many loving people, end up engulfed in loneliness? Why did they trust me? Maybe what I needed wasn't an office, but a Friendship Bench, like Zimbabwean communities where people who suffered from kufungisisa, a Shona word that meant' thinking too much', received help, not treatment, from grandmothers who volunteered to listen and offer relief through words."

I imagined her radiant voice like red velvet draped around her naked body, hiding a softness that only I could guess.

That last message sounded like a farewell, so I never bothered to reply. I called her mom once, but she said she hadn't heard from Katarina in a while.

Fractured lives

What took me back to Romania in June 2014 was the role of marriage reconciliation advisor my dad assigned to me. He called me in the middle of the night. Again.

"Ana, you need to come home. I'm getting a divorce," he yelled into the phone.

"Dad, calm down. It's three in the morning. I don't understand. What do you mean you're getting a divorce?"

"I'm leaving your mom. I don't love her anymore," he said.

I sat down on the storage bench at the end of my bed, ready to listen to a litany of complaints.

"Why would you care, anyway? Why would you understand? You just picked up your stuff and left. You never cared," he continued his monologue.

"I never said I didn't care. You always assume things about me. I'll call you back in the morning," I said.

After fifty years of marriage, two aging people were falling apart, going their different ways, taking all these memories away from me, the togetherness I had cherished in the stories that I told my friends, bragging about my parents' enduring relationship, about their resilience through times of fear, dictatorship, and gloom when they used to let down the dark wood stain blinds to listen to Radio Free Europe, a station banned in our country in the eighties.

"Don't tell anyone at school that we listen to this station," my dad warned us every time we huddled around an antique Gloria radio set that my mom had bought from a neighbour.

Were these the same people who taught me how to thunder through life without fear? Were these the same parents who preached the stability of marriage as if it had been a cocoon we wished to insulate our hearts in?

Now their marriage was like aged wallpaper coming off decrepit walls that neither of them cared to spruce up with a splash of colour. You could touch the loose edges, see the moisture patches left behind by the adhesive. Although my mom was still in the long-term care facility centre, to me, they were still a couple. Their life had completely changed, but I didn't expect my dad to give up on her so easily. They were still my parents, and I wanted to see them together.

I didn't want to call him back right away. I climbed in the middle of the bed, pulled the duvet over my head, and cried myself to sleep. When I woke up, I dialed his number. And I listened.

My dad had fallen in love with someone else. It happened when he read *Fractured Lives*, a book by a Romanian author. As he turned the last page, it felt like an invisible hand lifted the words off the page. They floated away, bigger and bigger until they got a life of their own. He could feel pain, love, confusion, and despair pouring out of him. He felt that, if he held out his hand, he could touch the writer's heart. He could feel the wounds carved into the story, caused by unspoken desires and forgotten dreams hidden behind simple words that had forced their existence into his mind like a drug that he refused to take.

This writer had come into my dad's life like a storm sweeping him off his feet, leaving him like a love-stricken teenager at a loss for words.

"I sat down and held my head in my hands for a few minutes, tuning out, rejecting the sun filtering through the sheer panels your mom bought on our twentieth wedding anniversary," he continued his story. "The familiar sounds and smells of the rooms I had lived in for so long felt foreign to me; I felt trapped, a prisoner of my own life. I went into the master bedroom, pulled out the navy-blue suitcase with scratched silver trim. Like a sleepwalker, I grabbed a few shirts, two pairs of pants, one belt, socks, some underwear, and threw them into the suitcase lying open on the bed. Your mom would have had a fit if she had been there. Every time we went away, she ironed and pressed all the clothes, tidily folded them up in two suitcases, equally divided should one get lost. She exasperated me with her neatness. The first thought that crossed my mind was how I was going to explain to you that I'd fallen under the spell of a young writer whose books kept me awake at night, haunted me, left me drained of energy, made me look at my aging body as if it didn't belong to me, as if my soul was held captive in someone else's sagging skin."

Would I ever understand and accept that my own dad, a man in his early seventies, discovered a sexuality that had repulsed him before? That he fell in love with a young man who could easily be his son? His name was Aron Tudose.

In September, just a couple of months after he broke the news to me, he moved in with his boyfriend. He took up exercising with a fervour that made him look like a billionaire septuagenarian in a cryogenic crypt. He completely changed his wardrobe and turned into a GAP skinny jeans fanatic. His partner wasn't so much into working out, but he was an avid runner who became an expert in navigating the narrow streets of Bucharest without getting into fights with angry drivers. Residential areas had morphed into deplorable parking lots that took away the pedestrians' right to enjoy their communities. Nothing intimidated him on his long runs.

"I can map out the city with my eyes closed," he said to me on the phone when I told him how impressed I was.

"In Canada, I need a GPS to get me even to the closest park," I said.

L'étage noble

Maria was born on October 28, 2014, a couple of weeks after Thanksgiving. A month later, I went back to Bucharest. *Bambini*. Why did they want to become parents at twenty-three? Why did they want to live in a city that offered no opportunities? An estranged city whose history was tainted by communist ideology birthed corrupt politicians who put themselves above the law.

I arrived on a dreary November afternoon. Before landing, I decided to ignore the rude agents who would check my passport.

"This way, Madam!" I heard a young voice. I didn't react.

"Excuse me, Madam! You can come this way," the young voice materialized in front of me, motioning me toward a booth with signage that read "Other countries". One line for EU citizens, one for diplomats and flight crews, and that one.

I smiled at him and replied in Romanian that I could wait in line.

Was that a cue that my country had changed for the better? That people were more trustful, kinder, more polite, less sneaky?

After a thirty-minute wait in a line crammed with tourists trying to push their overstuffed hand luggage on a semi-clean floor, I came to a desk that looked like a bar table behind which a young woman with fake eyelashes and heavy auburn hair was smiling at me. I thought I'd landed in the wrong airport or maybe she smiled at someone behind me. I turned, but the guy behind me was busy zipping his bags while a two-year-old clinging onto his pants was wiping off his boogers with the back of his sleeve. I looked back at the customs officer and stepped over the yellow line. She spoke to me in impeccable English, but switched to Romanian when she heard me speak.

I was out of the airport in less than an hour, which, even according to my standards, was a record.

I took a cab and give the driver the address.

"That's a nice area. Do you live there?" he asked.

"My son does," I said. "He bought an apartment on the top floor of a new building. A new subdivision, a mix of detached houses and low rises that are facing Herastrau Park. Apparently, his place is worth half a million euros. That's ridiculous. How did house prices rise so fast? When I lived here, a five hundred square foot apartment wasn't more than fifty-thousand euros."

"What year was that?" the driver asked, raising his eyebrows.

He looked very young, maybe in his mid-twenties; dark hair, a thick black mustache that reminded me of Movember posters in Canada.

"That must have been in 2000," I said thinking of the many times I had gone back to Romania since I left in 1990.

All these memories came to me like a big, unexpected wave on a still lake, shaking my boat, making me lose my balance. I remembered my old neighbourhood, a typical byproduct of the communist construction boom: clusters of high-rise buildings with matchbox apartments where large families shared the coveted living space.

Our building had been left unfinished, its U-shaped design that was meant to create a sense of enclosure made it look like a war-torn zone where the sides revealed only metal rods protruding from gravel-filled basements, a hide-and-seek heaven for children. Kids on my block used to tell stories about a cemetery that used to be on the same land. When some of my friends' grandparents died, everyone believed it was because of the curse put on developers by the dead or by family members who had to deal with their remains dug out by excavators and backhoe loaders. The smell of death never went away.

It was the first time when my trip didn't turn into a disillusioned journey into the past, sprinkled with over-priced dinners at exclusive restaurants where I was the only one who spoke Romanian.

Instead of X-raying the city for lifestyle ulcers and political tumors, I focused my energy on Matthew and his family. As a first-time mom, Julia was managing better than I expected, all the breastfeeding, the diaper changing, the waking up during the night routine. She never complained, she didn't look tired, she was composed, grounded, present. Something I wasn't when Matthew was a baby.

"Ana, I'm so happy you're here," she said as soon as I arrived. "You don't need to do anything, just be with us. I can handle the baby."

They gave me the spare room that was also an office, so they had to move their shared desk into the kitchen. Their apartment had a relaxed look created through a mix of contemporary and coastal décor that fit their lifestyle. Neutral colour furniture pieces accented with bright-embroidered cushions, large abstract artwork displayed next to marine landscapes, bowls of seashells, and miniature wooden ships.

"It's our imaginary beach house," Julia said. "One day, we'll build a small cottage by the Black Sea, on Ovidiu Island, less than half an hour away from Constanța."

Matthew shared my love for being close to the water, so it didn't surprise me. But Ovidiu Island? Why not one of the more popular destinations like Mamaia or Costinești?

Julia didn't change too much since the Thanksgiving dinner when I had first met her back in Canada. Motherhood added a sensual fullness to her body without ruining her statuesque presence. Her guarded deference toward me made me wonder whether she knew how mad I was when Matthew decided to leave Canada. Even if she knew, she never alluded to it, proving again I was the one who overreacted.

One night, I offered to watch Maria while they went out. It took some convincing as Matthew believed it would interfere with my plans. What plans? I was there for them, not for me.

"Mom, I'm not sure if I want you to do that. I mean, not because I don't trust you, but I want you to relax. This is too much work," Matthew said.

"For my age, you mean. Hey, I'm not that old, you know that. Besides, I'll blame you for becoming a grandmother at forty-nine."

"Ana, please don't hold her all the time. I know how grandmas are. We don't want her to be spoiled. Please?" Julia said.

Of course, I was going to hold her all the time. Why not? They eventually agreed and left me in charge.

Maria was a quiet baby who cried only when she was hungry or needed a diaper change. The rest of the time she either napped or stared at black and white geometric shapes taped on her crib rails.

I moved the printed sheets on the couch, and I held her in my arms all the time. Rocked her, held her, kissed her. I lay down and put her on my belly, her walnut-sized head resting on my left breast, her rapid shallow breaths being the only noise in the room. We both fell asleep, each dreaming her own dreams, two generations apart, in a country that we both called home.

The week spent with them was my vacation that year. Dad called several times, but I refused to see him.

"Mom, I don't understand why you're so stubborn. He's still your dad," Matthew said.

In my books, he wasn't. He was no longer the dad I remembered.

For Matthew's sake, I agreed to see him and his partner Aron who had become a sensation in the Romanian landscape of contemporary fiction. His latest book, the same one that fascinated my dad, explored so many polarizing ideas that dominated the society and ignited younger generations' civic engagement: hate speech, politicians' false promises, active participation in building a true democracy, and freedom of sexual orientation. His characters were young hipsters living in historic residential neighbourhoods like Floreasca and Mântuleasa, formerly inhabited by communist leaders whose ghost stories continued to cast a shadow over Bucharest. His take, though, wasn't one of anger or remorse, but of revival and hope. When I read his book, I understood why my dad liked him. Aron was able to reimagine a city through the eyes of two young males, Dan and Pavel, university graduates with dreams of becoming professors, who spent their money on a grassroots movement called *Today's Romania – We Care* that promoted local arts and culture, honouring iconic Romanian actors, sponsoring young directors to produce films that reflected Romanian values, and organizing book clubs that propelled local writers onto the international scene.

His generous acceptance of a flawed country fighting to redeem itself was unexpected, especially given his age. Most of his friends, in their late twenties and early thirties, had left the country in search of a new identity, chasing the chimera of a better life in cities whose walls enclosed a richer history narrated in a language that gave a new dimension to their ambitions.

It was hard not to love him. At six foot two, with dark curly hair, and a smile that was impossible to fake, Aron was one of those people whose simple presence in a room was like a light that attracted the crowd. At book-signing events, he hugged everyone, wrote long personalized messages, asked about his readers' significant others and their reading preferences, listened to their opinions, shook their hands, and ran around the room like a child opening his Christmas presents.

"You know, Ana, he's the first man I've ever met who has never talked badly about anyone. He's so happy, so positive, so accepting of others' imperfections, that I almost believe he's not real," my dad said.

I could see how Aron had such an impact on my dad's life. He was like a patch of green grass on barren land; miracle, hope, and light all in one place. And Dad was the lucky one who chose to enjoy it without any guilt.

"You should come for dinner one night. I'll cook cabbage rolls for you," he said.

That was an image I could not reconcile: a young successful writer preoccupied with arts and literature hunched over cabbage leaves, mixing long grain rice and sautéed onion with ground meat. But I decided to go.

They lived in a two-storey apartment close to University Square. The 1960s building that featured an elevator perfectly fit inside an oak spiral staircase was nicknamed the *Hausmannian*, referencing the signature architecture of Paris known for its massive cut stone blocks.

When I arrived, Dad answered the door and told me Aron was busy in the kitchen. I waved at him as he dragged me up the stairs.

"Let me show you the library," Dad said.

The second floor, which Aron ironically called *l'étage noble*, was one big room that stored only books, works of art, a loveseat, and a desk. Over two thousand books were stacked on high shelves, on the floor, in hanging baskets pinned to the walls, in large glass vases, and even in ceramic pots. The oil portrait paintings, signed by a Romanian contemporary artist, looked like tortured men and women whose smudged faces resembled claw scratches of wild animals. Faces screaming in pain, eyes hidden by bandages or clay masks, half-torn arms dangling from mold-coloured walls, dark shadows casting on ivory doors floating in the air.

"What do you think, huh? What do you think? Do you like it? Tell me, do you like it?" Dad said.

"Yes, Dad, I do. I do like it," I said. "Let's go downstairs and see if Aron needs help."

The cabbage rolls were better than I expected. How could he cook so well? When did he have time to learn?

I never went to their house after that. Several times, we met in the historic district, for a quick dessert or an espresso on patios with large white cushioned chairs, surrounded by expats and young artists.

A slice of life

My mom's health deteriorated quickly. After Dad moved in with his partner Aron, we relocated her from Snagov to another long-term care facility in Câmpina called *A Slice of Life*, one hundred kilometres away from Bucharest. Their website promised residents a life full of joy in a facility built in the heart of nature. Fragrant false acacia and linden trees lined up the main alley, and a small pond in the lush backyard offered an unobstructed view of the forest behind. Hundred-year-old evergreen trees completed the postcard image.

They promised an abundance of community re-engagement activities that would help with her recovery, but she wasn't able to enjoy any of them. Due to her limited mobility and loss of speech, she was a perfect candidate for around-the-clock medical care. She went through countless hours of speech and physical therapy, without real progress. Every time I saw her, she looked even more lost in her own world, a landscape governed by silent stories, hand squeezes, and forgiving smiles. She recognized me, but she showed little interest in what I was saying. After a few minutes of intently fixing her eyes on me, she would wave in exhaustion like a teacher ready to dismiss her class.

"I'm done with you," she seemed to say. "Leave me alone."

She never tried to speak. I was the one doing all the talking, laughing at my own jokes, stirring up memories that I hoped would bring her back from no man's land, asking for her opinion on topics that lacked relevance, if she believed Katarina was really my best friend, or if Keeran and I would ever get back together. I learned to interpret her silences, hand movements, or oblique looks in a manner that suited me.

At first, Dad visited her every weekend. As he got busy with Aron and their projects, his trips to *A Slice of Life* got rarer and rarer.

"I can't believe you're doing this to her," I said when I met him and Aron for coffee one day. "Is this what your life with her amounts to? Awkward visits that you hope will be as short as possible?"

He just sat there, playing with the saucer, lifting his espresso cup and putting it down without drinking, wiping imaginary crumbs off the table, shifting in his chair as if his weight had been too much for such a flimsy piece of furniture. Aron was an uninvited witness to a family scene that wasn't supposed to happen.

Every time I went back to see her, she seemed less aware, frailer, more detached from her surroundings. None of my stories cheered her up. I made fun of Dad and his outings with Aron to clubs and cafés packed with twenty-year-olds, I gave her detailed reports about my life alone, about my fear Matthew wouldn't be able to adapt to Romania, about my worry Katarina would never return from India. All my attempts at making her participate in the conversation or at least disagree with me drew a blank stare. Nothing seemed to move on the inside.

Physically, she was there, but her brain refused to make the connections that made her my mom. The unique connections that made her say the right words, do the right movements, or show the right emotion in a context that elicited a reaction from her. She was and she wasn't. She wasn't there. But she was still my mom.

I checked out other centres closer to Bucharest. The train ride to Câmpina was too much of a hassle. A couple of places that an acquaintance had recommended were run by former leaders of the Communist Party and charged double for fewer services. I decided not to move her and take days one at a time, a cliché that had started to carve a different meaning since her stroke. Each day gave me a chance to celebrate her, to love her, to share memories that she could no longer understand, to tell her about my marriage that she could no longer remember – that I could no longer remember – to ask her questions that she would never answer, to tell her stories that I would eventually forget.

Together & alone

Matthew and Julia got very close to Dad and Aron. Whenever I called, he told me he was going over to Dad's for dinner, or that they were going to the movies, and Aron was watching Maria, or that they were going on a ski trip to Braşov together. There was always an event, an outing, a gathering that involved Dad and his newly found world of young writers, emerging artists, and hipsters.

"You're going skiing? Dad doesn't even know how to ski. Is it even safe at his age?"

"Mom, you're so over-protective. Even with your own dad. That's weird. Besides, he does know how to ski. Anyway, I've got to go. We're running late for Aron's reading event. I'll talk to you later."

Partying together, cooking together, travelling together, reading together. They created their enclosed universe of get-togethers with its own set of rules, inside jokes, and newly built family memories. They explored the historic district, went shopping to luxury malls, joined Aron for literary events at Cărtureşti bookstore, and escaped the big city to B&Bs in bucolic places like Moieciu or Viscri where even Prince Charles had built a guesthouse.

Matthew's job rarely required travel, and the short trips he had to take to Prague, Amsterdam, or Munich, gave him and Julia an excuse for romantic getaways while Maria stayed with Aron and Dad.

"Matthew, are you sure they can take care of a baby? Aron is so young, and Dad is not really in his prime. Do you trust them?"

"Mom, you worry too much. As usual. We're fine. Everyone's fine. Aron and Grandpa are the perfect babysitters: caring, available, eager to help. You should come over. Take some time off and we can all go on a trip. Maybe to a place in Romania you have never visited or one that you cherish."

I did want to visit a special place, but not with them. What were we now? An extended family of loving people, sharing memories, and planning trips together?

I thought about going back to the place where my parents took me after I finished grade eight. It was their present for passing my high school entrance exam with high grades. It was a small town in Maramureş, Sighetu Marmației, a region frozen in time, where life revolved around the village church. Although my family wasn't religious, they paid respect to a community that organized their life events in the wooden churches known for their high roofs and pointed steeples. The area attracted many tourists, both from Romania and abroad, who were curious about the blue wooden crosses in the Merry Cemetery, known for its funny epitaphs engraved on colourful tombstones.

One of the reasons why I wished to see that place again was because it reminded me of a time when my future was predictable – finish high school, go to University of Bucharest, become a teacher and, with a little bit of luck, receive a job assignment at one of the middle schools in the suburbs, like all university graduates during the Communist regime. You didn't pick where to work. They chose it for you. The party. The government. It was a well-oiled machine of party leaders sealing everyone's fate through decrees, orders, and appointments – all working like clockwork in turning people into obedient, mindless beings, happy to accept their destiny.

Running out of time

It was three in the morning when Dad called me from Brussels where he had accompanied Aron to a two-day writers' conference.

"Ana, you need to go to Bucharest. Your mom had another stroke. Things don't look good," he said.

"Are you coming?"

"No, I can't. I promised Aron we're going to Bruges."

"Are you out of your mind? Did you just say you're going to Bruges? What happened to you?"

"Sorry, Ana. I have to go," he said, hanging up.

He had to go. He promised his partner. He had an excuse. He was busy. He had his own life. I didn't. His wife for over fifty years was fighting for her life on a bed in a sanitized building ironically called *A Slice of Life*, and he didn't care. Or maybe he did, and I was the one who could no longer grasp the meaning of words. Simple words that were meant to tell the truth. Leathery words like firefly wings lighting up the sky on a summer night. Words that travelled through the air leaving behind distorted sounds of pain, landing into my ear with a crash – thump, smack, thisshig rrrerrk – like a broken loudspeaker.

I had been ready for this moment since I arrived in Canada, just like pregnant women get their bags ready for the hospital well before their due date. A few changes of clothes, travel toiletries, my passport, some cash, a black dress. The Air Canada flight pass that I had saved since my mom's first stroke came in handy. I booked my flight the same day and, by six in the evening, I boarded a plane to Bucharest with a connecting flight in Paris.

This time, it wasn't New Year's Eve, but the atmosphere still looked festive; a care-free, holiday-like chatter that reminded me of Sunwing champagne flights. Smiling flight attendants, overjoyed kids who kept switching seats with their parents to better see the clouds, young couples cradling babies to sleep before placing them in the baskets in front of them, each family insulated in their own bubble. Mine had collapsed and then crumbled into tiny fragments that retained only a slight resemblance to its former sturdiness. My only shield against all the conviviality around me was a pair of old headphones that I kept on for the entire duration of the flight.

After landing in Bucharest, I picked up a rental car and drove to the Municipal Hospital in Câmpina where my mom was on life support. The doctor on duty spent two minutes with me, explaining that they couldn't do anything more for someone like her who had a massive hemorrhagic stroke. Because the nurse didn't call the doctor immediately, they were not able to control the bleeding, which caused severe brain damage.

"Miss, the likelihood of recovery is zero; our efforts to provide care would be a waste of resources. We should take her off life support. No brain activity. Zero. No thoughts. This is no longer your mother. It's just a body in a coma. She will never come out of it. I'll give you fifteen minutes and then I'll come back to discuss," he said.

Wait, that guy gave me a quarter of an hour to make an end-of-life choice for my own mother? No brain activity? What was he talking about? What did that even mean?

I lay down next to her and hugged her tightly. She had been reduced to an amorphous shape, light and airy, with skeletal hands sticking out from under the blanket. Only her face had the same marshmallowy softness that I remembered from the butterfly kisses she gave me when I was a little girl. Her heartbeat was just a flutter, like an injured bird flapping her wings in a desperate attempt to fly. I knew how to rescue a bird in distress; all I had to do was place her in a quiet and dark place, give her time to recuperate. Keep her safe. Let her rest. I didn't know how to save my mom. How to keep her safe. I wasn't going to cry. She knew I was there, and I didn't want to remember myself that way. Instead, I put my lips to her right ear and whispered memories that had been buried for so long.

"Do you remember my seventh-grade graduation ceremony? When I won the academic excellence award. You kneeled on stage and hugged me in front of the entire school. I was so embarrassed. Do you remember when I went on a school trip to Braşov and I refused to wear the pants that you bought me only because they were not my favourite colour? Will you ever forget the moments when I didn't want you to be my mom, when I didn't confide in you like other teenage girls did, when I told my friends I was an orphan, when I wanted only Dad to come to the parent-teacher interviews? Will you ever forgive me for not being the daughter that you wanted me to be? For

205

not thanking you enough, for not loving you more, for not being there when you needed me?

I feel like I'm running out of time. And so are you. You gave birth to me and now I am the one who will decide whether you should be taken off life support. How ironic is that, Mom? You gave me life and I give you death. I bet that's not what you had in mind when you decided to have a child. I don't want to be the one who has the final word. I wish Dad were here. Stay with me, don't go. Can you squeeze my hand if you hear me? Please? You can't, can you? Why didn't you call me or have someone call me if you didn't feel well? You couldn't. I know. What am I saying? But even if you could, you wouldn't have done it. You're too proud, I know. I would have done the same. I'm not blaming you. I'm just trying to understand. What happened to you and Dad, anyway? What happened to him? Moving in with that young man! That's pathetic. Don't get me wrong, and sorry for saying that, I really like the guy. He's smart and funny, and well-read, and fit, and quite good-looking. I don't know what attracted him to Dad. This is so wrong. On so many levels. Anyway, who cares, right? You are here, alone, I mean not alone-alone, you're with me, but you know, you are without him, without a man who can tell you he loves you. Wait, I'm not making too much sense. I can tell you I love you. I mean there's no man in your life who can tell you that you matter, that your life matters. If you want to know, I was so mad at him. I still am. And now, he had the nerve to tell me he was busy. Fathom that! Dad, busy. Busy with what, I meant to ask. But I didn't. I let it go. Can you imagine me doing that? Letting go? I had to learn how to let go. Especially after my divorce. I know what you think. That was a long time ago and I should move on. Should have moved on. But I couldn't, Mom. I simply couldn't. I tried, believe me. Well, at least, I had Matthew. It was worth it. Are you thirsty? Do you want some water? Mom, can you hear me? I'll go get some water."

I left the room only for a couple of minutes. When I returned, the doctor was there, standing by the bed, checking his charts, and looking intently at the machines.

"Well, Miss. What did you decide? I can't stay here too long. I have other patients to tend to."

In his mid-thirties, with a Pompadour haircut, blue eyes, and a light tan, the doctor who didn't introduce himself looked more like a professional vacationer off to a Caribbean beach to enjoy cocktails garnished with mini umbrellas.

There was a disconnect between that image and him being near dying patients, and dealing with family members in denial, or writing prescriptions to ailing seniors.

"I need a few more minutes, please. I want to call my dad," I said.

"Okay, I'll be back in ten,"

I called my dad, but he didn't answer. I knew he wouldn't. Why did I even try? Why wasn't I surprised?

I got to the age when I started being surrounded by death. Parents, friends, uncles, aunts, they seemed to have aged overnight, their frail bodies making room for emptiness, one cell at a time.

I hadn't been there to see those changes in my mom. But I imagined that, at first, it was her facial expression. It lost luminosity. Her eyes turned into dried out wells. Ghosts of twinkle that once made someone's heart race. Then, the colouring. She got paler and paler until she started resembling a corpse, and, if I had been next to her, I could have hardly controlled my itch to pinch her cheeks to make her blush again. After that, it was her body odour. Her favourite fragrance of lavender and honey that always reminded me of summer sunsets in a violet shimmering field faded away as the smell of death took hold of her diminished body.

I knew sickness and death touched people in different ways. When it was someone close to us, the avalanche of emotions – denial, frustration, helplessness – paralyzed us. How could I accept that I wasn't able to miraculously heal her or somehow bring her back to life, to her former self?

I looked out the small window covered with a white embroidered curtain as I sat down on the bed. The only sound in the room was the heartbeat coming from the life support machine.

* * *

"Dad, she's gone. Mom passed away. I mean, I decided to take her off life support. Service will be in two days, so I thought you wanted to know. Are you coming home?" I told him on the phone.

"Sorry, honey, I can't. We're busy with Aron's tour. You can handle that, right? I must go. Take care."

You're busy?? Are you asking me if I can handle it? Are we really having this conversation? Am I living in an upside-down world where basic feelings for someone who has been your partner for half a century have disappeared? Vanished. Gone. As if that life didn't exist. Just like Keeran. Not one whom I could trust.

Dad refused to come, but his partner sent flowers.

After she had her first stroke, I secretly kept a white candle and an icon of the Virgin Mary in my purse. Although my mom had not been superstitious, in her late years, like an omen, she kept talking about how people who died in the dark would end in hell. As if the light of a dollar store candle were meant to illuminate her path into the afterlife.

My mother was an occasional churchgoer, just like social smokers. She believed in the power of redemption measured only by the amount of time that one spent praying on their knees in front of the altar. Therefore, she never considered herself worthy of God's attention when it came to services that the church might or should deliver on her behalf. Despite that, and unfamiliar with the actual ritual, I decided to offer her a traditional funeral after I spoke with Aunt Valeria and Uncle Petru, the only two family members who offered to help. Religion hadn't been instrumental in the lives of most people in my parents' generation, but necessary, present in three forms that marked key life stages – baptisms, weddings, burials – so, a religious service was more like an act of bringing her into the fold.

I was able to secure a service at St. Spiridon Church, the largest in Bucharest, after many hours of negotiating with a funeral home, an obnoxious Orthodox priest who commanded his fee in unequivocal terms, and an army of church staff.

Funeral homes were a new concept that emerged in post-communist Romania, some of them replicating business models run in Germany or Austria, countries that Romanians travelled to in the first years after the borders opened. They took care of everything; I didn't have to worry about whether I followed the tradition or broke any sacraments dictated by the Orthodox Church. My only assignment was to get new clothes and shoes for the burial, along with an anointed holy icon that was to be placed on the coffin.

Many of my parents' neighbours joined us for a memorial service where Aunt Valeria gave a brief speech about Mom's last years of life haunted by a loss of memory and then of speech. I would have added another loss, but I didn't want to attract everyone's attention to the fact that my dad was missing. A few collages of family pictures assembled in a hurry and pinned on the walls amongst sacred images of saints completed the service. I could no longer cry. The open casket revealed a waxy face I couldn't recognize. That wasn't how I wanted to remember her.

Some of the neighbours commented on my dad's choice to get a divorce with the aplomb that made them sound like family counselling experts.

"Tsk-tsk, what a shame. At his age, to do that... I mean, leave your mom, and the other thing, you know. That's a disgrace for your family. Sorry to say that. But what came over him? Such a beautiful wife, they lived together for so many years," said an older woman whose name I couldn't remember.

"Ana, she's right. It's none of my business, but what's wrong with him? He did that to your mom. I would never forgive him if I were you," another one said.

"Don't worry, I didn't, I won't," I said to everyone's satisfaction.

"I hope he at least lit a candle when he heard she'd passed away," I heard someone else voicing their opinion.

"Ana, don't you have a son? Was it too much for him to travel?", another neighbour asked.

"He actually lives here now."

"Oh, my God! And he didn't even bother to come? Oh, wow, oh, I didn't know."

"Ana, people will think you don't care," Aunt Valeria said to me. "I didn't see a tear in your eyes."

Why did more tears mean more empathy or pain? She was the one who didn't understand. All those long nights worrying about the phone ringing, the shocking news about Dad's affair and separation, my mom's pain, her loneliness, her alienation, everything was incongruent with the image I had of my family. All my memories of them together disintegrated into flashes of light and darkness like shadows of silhouettes dancing, projected on barren walls; coming together and growing apart, until all I could see were two black lines smudged onto the harsh surface.

Before we took her to the chapel, several women who lived in the same apartment building as my parents took the reins of the ceremony and guided us through the progression of the event. Their advice, a mixture of pagan and Christian elements, was received with reverence only by a couple of older people, while the rest laughed it off.

"Ana, you must pull a strand of her hair and place it on the door; it's for good luck… or maybe for keeping evil spirits away? I don't remember, but it doesn't matter why, you must do it," one of the ad-hoc funeral managers shared her superstition.

"No, you're wrong," another well-meaning friend jumped in. "You need to put the hair on the window ledge."

"You are wrong. How did you come up with that? I bet you don't know about the handkerchiefs that must be handed out to mourners. Ana, did you buy handkerchiefs?" another one said.

Although I did my best to entertain all of them, it was beyond my understanding how they all turned into emcees of a performance whose protagonist left the stage without saying good-bye. They kept the show going by switching roles, becoming the main characters in a religious ceremony whose sanctity was tarnished by the bickering over who should hand out the handkerchiefs. It looked like a play within a play, reminding me of Tom Stoppard's *The Real Inspector Hound*. Mere spectators accidentally pulled onto the stage by an event that turned them into actors. We each had our own soliloquy, followed by brief dialogues that were not exactly a true exchange of information since we were all too anxious to give advice, share our opinions, judge, and label everyone else. Atheists, agnostics, and believers were all giving in to superstitions to accommodate a bunch of senile friends. In the chaos that erupted after the wake when every single person claimed religious authority, I managed to reach the priest and asked him to take control of the situation. When the wake was over, everyone followed him out of the church in a quiet procession toward the grave, the cross carriers in front leading the way for the pallbearers.

I observed the cortege as if I were a stranger who happened to be present at an event that had nothing to do with me. What came to mind were descriptions of near-death experiences when the victim felt they had left their body which they observed from above. I let myself float over the mourners, as light as air, searching for the open grave in the distance. It was a small cemetery in a residential area, surrounded by poplars and oak trees, with potted plants along the alleyway, and a few landscaped graves that must have been the VIP section. It took us less than five minutes to get to it. A hole in the ground like a dark crater that would swallow the wooden coffin in no time. The chanting words of the priest who swung his censer like a pendulum somehow reached my mind as a melody enshrouded in sadness. An incessant humming pierced my eardrums, dissolving the sounds into music. The fragrance of burnt incense made me nauseous. I watched how the women surrounded the grave held hands and recited the Lord's Prayer with a fervour meant to forgive the deceased of all sins.

I couldn't watch her coffin being lowered into the grave. The last memory of her that I wanted to carry in my heart was of a happy woman wearing a floral print dress, holding my hands and dancing with me in a circle singing a nursery rhyme that sounded like *Ring a Round o' Roses*.

Valeria and Petru offered to help me with the sale of my parents' apartment, but I declined. Their job was done. I wanted them gone. No more family meddling in my affairs. Dad was quick in giving me power of attorney, which was required for the sale, and said he didn't need anything. How generous of him! How thoughtful! It took me less than two weeks to sell their place to a young couple starting a family. I let the bank worry about the money transfer into my Canadian account and booked my flight back to Toronto, leaving behind my raggedy past like a lizard shedding its skin.

After the funeral, I brought back to Canada an old-fashioned suitcase made of pigskin leather that my mom had inherited from her parents. I stuffed it with family pictures and a few handicraft items: intricately hand-painted Easter eggs, colour glazed ceramic pots decorated with geometric shapes, a miniature hand-carved wooden tree of life from the Merry Cemetery in Săpânța, and a couple of hand-blown glass vases. I kept the pictures in the antique valise, but I spread the souvenirs around the house like trophies that celebrated my mother's life and the anticipation of better days for me.

Dad never called after that. And I didn't bother to get in contact with him. What kind of man was he? What kind of husband did he become in the late years with my mom? What kind of person did he turn into not to care about her, about me?

I spent the whole month of January fantasizing about gold-sand beaches and Caribbean mojitos. Like never before, winter felt like an interminable series of freezing rain and snow pellets pounding down on icy sidewalks. I traded my daily strolls for short bursts of treadmill runs at the gym, which I hated.

Katarina emailed me from India to tell me she was coming back. Not sure when. But she was. The news of her return threw me in a frenzy of preparation although I didn't know the exact date. Should I cook her favourite dish? Wait, what was her favourite dish? Should I wait for her at the airport? Should I call her mom and go together? Should I offer her the spare bedroom which used to be Matthew's? What should I wear?

At work, I was busier than ever. The agency had taken on several more clients that were more demanding than we anticipated.

My boss expected me to be a project manager, creative director, account manager, and counsellor. No questions asked. It didn't bother me. The extra hours spent in the office meant I wasn't home alone, eating dinner out of a shoddy take-out box while watching CTV News.

When I got home in the evening it looked like my entire neighbourhood had signed a secret pact to keep all the lights out, which made my street look like a scene from a war movie where everyone ran for shelter. It turned into a city under siege whose residents lived under curfew. As gloomy as it looked, I liked the quietude of the dark houses sunken into a deep slumber.

Suspended in time, living in a place that rarely looked inhabited gave my life a transient feeling that helped me avoid any serious talk with Matthew who called every other day.

"Mom, please come and live with us. I'm sure you can find a job here if you want. You've stayed in touch with some of your old friends, right?"

"I don't know. I don't know. It's not that easy."

"But it is. It is easy. You are the one who overcomplicates it. You can live with us."

Live with them? In that tiny apartment? I didn't think so.

"That would be too much for your family, Matthew. Let me mull this over. If I ever decide to move back, I want to have my own place."

No one will remember you

Here I am. After twenty-five years of drifting memories. Ending what felt like an overdue pregnancy. Delivering my progeny to the world. No more excuses. No more pain. Only relief, light, hope. And the premonition of love.

I've rehearsed the acceptance speech in my head many times, but every time I say it out loud, it doesn't sound right. I wish Keeran were here. He would know what to do. What to say. How to say it. Why am I even thinking of him? Didn't I learn my lesson? What's wrong with me for Chrissake?

I wave at my neighbour who's playing hockey with his daughter in the driveway. Doesn't he see that I'm no longer just Ana Owen? I want him to stop whatever he's doing with his puck, and ask me questions, assure me that the award that I'm going to receive tonight is the only way of reclaiming my identity. He points at the clouds instead, mimicking the act of hara-kiri with his stick.

An ash sky glides over Mississauga like a wobbly giant spreading a mort cloth on a coffin. No one has seen the sun for a week, which has generated a slew of articles about the despondency of February blues and why Canadians experience seasonal affective disorders more than any other nation. After so many winters, I start feeling it, too. But I don't care what the weather is like, what coping mechanism I could learn to fight the winter blahs, what country I live in, what time it is. Because nothing is going to spoil the evening of my life. Nothing is going to take this moment away.

I turn on the radio. Another weather report. "*It looks like February 2015 will be Toronto's coldest month in recorded history. Despite the ridiculous cold, people still flock to the beaches to do selfies with nature's ice sculptures. In the past thirty-seven frigid days, the daily high never broke the melting point...*" I don't want to listen to weather forecasts. Despite the freezing temperatures, I feel like rolling down the windows on my green Ford Escape to cruise along the Queen Elizabeth Way (QEW) like a teenager who stole her parents' car, eager to show the world that she's in charge.

The vibration of my iPhone buried in the Braun Büffel purse, interrupts my reverie. I rummage through the bag, and I pull it out, veering into the emergency lane for a quick second.

"Matthew, I'm on my way. I'm passing Spadina as we speak. I should be there in ten minutes."

"Mom, don't rush, you have plenty of time... Mom? I'm very proud of you!"

"Oh, thanks, honey. What time did you get there?"

Nothing.

"Hello? Hello...?"

He hung up on me. Again.

The awards ceremony is at seven o'clock, but I want to be there early.

It's the first time that the event has been postponed to February due to some judging panel changes. I wish it were done in October, as usual. Matthew and I could have gone for a long walk on Lakeshore.

I take the Bay Street exit from the Gardiner Expressway and drive on Queens Quay West toward Simcoe Street. I park in P3 on Reese Street and walk to the main entrance of the Harbourfront Centre to meet him.

He's pacing back and forth, talking on his phone, gesticulating, laughing, waving at me. When I get closer, he puts his phone away and gives me a hug.

"Hi, Mom, I'm sorry I couldn't come home first."

Of course, he's not. He's been living seven thousand kilometres away for quite some time, so I'm no longer sure I know where his home is.

"That's okay. You're not late. What happened?"

"My connecting flight in Munich was delayed, so I arrived late in Toronto. I hope you don't mind", he says, grabbing my arm like his father used to.

"That's fine, honey. I'm so happy you could make it," I say.

I wonder why he came alone.

As if he had read my mind, he says, "Julia couldn't come. You know Maria got another ear infection. Right after her first birthday, the pediatrician recommended tubes, but we're not so sure that will help. I mean, you know she wished she could come. Well… Mom, you…here… winning this award. I'm so surprised. And proud of you. I can't wait to hear all about it."

I squeeze his arm. We keep walking. The wind whips my face like sharp blades of pampas grass that crack my skin open. I pull my wool scarf over my half-frozen cheeks.

"For years and years, all I can remember about my life was work, work, work, chores, and more work. I rarely found the

218

time to just sit down, gather my thoughts, see what truly moved me, what made me go. When I met your dad, I felt like a character in Camil Petrescu's *The Last Night of Love, The First Night of War*, hoping that "lacking any special talents and not believing in God, the only way for me to be happy would be to find perfect love." It wasn't meant to be that way. So, I had to find my happiness somewhere else. I had so many friends who encouraged me to go for it." I say looking at him.

"Anyway, I did it for every woman who made the choices that I made, every mother who worried to death for her children, every wife who second-guessed herself, every displaced individual who moved to a country without memories."

"That sounds like you, Mom", Matthew says. "Is that how you felt when you moved to Canada?"

I look up at the Porter airplanes flying low, getting ready to land on Toronto Island.

"You should have flown to Billy Bishop instead of Pearson!" I say.

"Mom, you know there are no direct flights from Europe."

"You're right. I forgot."

"Mom, are you hungry?" Matthew asks.

I stop mid-step and look at him as if I forgot he was here. Things happened so fast. I'm happy he came, but I don't know how to tell him I'm sorry.

"I am," I say.

"We have enough time for a quick bite and a beer. Let's go to Amsterdam Brew House; it's close."

Time, time. Everyone thinks they have time for everything. They live as if they had all the time in the world. Especially Matthew.

Anyway, it's only a few minutes away.

We head north on Lower Simcoe and turn left on Queens Quay to get to the pub. The place is empty, but it's going to be packed in a couple of hours. We sit at the bar and order an artichoke and spinach dip, and two Creemore Springs on tap.

I look around at the few people sitting next to us. A young couple are holding hands for a few minutes, then the woman, with her head slightly tilted, ostentatiously twists her diamond and amethyst ring while the man who seems to be her fiancé strokes her hair. Their gestures recall images of love and desire in Renaissance art, of painters who obsessively try to capture the elusiveness of their lovers' naked bodies.

At a different table, there are two young men, one of them protectively leaned over, scribbling down some notes on a piece of paper that partially covers the title of the book underneath "Editing Canadian English, ... edition". I smile at a scene that looks so familiar.

I drink my warm beer and think of Keeran as this was something that drove him crazy.

"Casting pearls before swine," he said the first time I asked for one.

I dip the toasted pita into the artichoke and then enjoy my drink.

The first time I drank warm beer was on a trip to London. I thought it was a joke when a friend said I should try it.

Matthew's glass is still full.

"What's on your mind, honey?" I ask.

"Nothing… It's just… I don't know. It's silly, I know, but I miss Julia and Maria. Is that weird?" he says.

"Yes, it's weird. I'm just kidding. It's not. Of course, it's not. It's perfectly normal."

Is it?

"Mom, do you remember how we made up stories when I was little? How each of us took turns and you told me Romanian folk tales before I went to bed?"

"I do," I say.

I smile at him, wondering which stories he remembers. I remember all of them.

"I remember. Those moments kept me going. When I felt I stepped out of my life, into a world where everything was possible."

I used storytelling as an excuse to tell stupid jokes and be silly.

"I still remember the story about the little boy who took out a permanent marker and coloured all his body in blue," he says.

"It feels like yesterday. I can see the dimples in your cheeks. You giggled a lot. You must admit that one was the stupidest. 'And a little girl said he should take a bath in orange juice, and someone else said he should wash it off with coffee, and another said he should bathe in milk.' We went on and on until you fell asleep."

"It's time to sleep, it's time to sleep,

The fishes croon in waters deep.

The songbirds sing in trees above

It's time to sleep, my love, my love."

Images of Matthew's curly hair hidden under the duvet as we played peekaboo, a prelude to our storytelling ritual, stir up memories that I cannot forget.

Looking around the pub, I notice how much it's changed since my last visit. The taps at the bar have multiplied over the years, making room for the local craft beers like Mill Street Organic and Conductor's Craft Ale.

"Excuse me, ma'am, do you speak German by any chance?" a gray-haired man with a bushy mustache asks me as he tries to sit at our table.

Matthew leans toward me, covering half of the table, rearranging the appetizer plates and cutlery.

"No, I don't, I'm sorry," I say looking at Matthew.

"I saw your Braun Büffel purse, I know you can get it only in Germany, and I thought…I'm sorry, I'm really sorry," he says going back to his table.

We both burst into laughter, feeling bad for the poor guy who must be feeling lonely, looking for someone who shared his past, a familiarity that I've craved since I lost contact with people who spoke my own language.

"We should get going," I say, getting my purse.

The German guy looking for a friend reminds me of Karl, the guy from work whom I thought liked me, but nothing really happened between us.

As he goes back to his table, I watch him walk; the same waddle, the swaying of arms that almost knock over the cutlery placed at the edge of the table, the same clumsiness. He moves into the far-right side of the booth where neither I, nor Matthew can see him.

I don't know what time it is. What if we're running late? What if they started the ceremony earlier?

When Matthew's phone rings, I know it's Julia. When he takes it out, I can hear Maria's voice.

"Daddy, where are you? I miss you. I can't sleep. Please tell me one of your stories, from your head," she says.

I smile as Matthew starts making up a story "from his head" to help her fall asleep.

The same ritual he and I had when he was little. But this time, he's not with her, he cannot snuggle up with her like we used to. He cannot hold his daughter close to him, stroke her hair, or give her a million kisses. He takes out a pencil and a notepad from his bag and starts doodling. What is he doing?

"Mom, how old was I when we moved back to Romania? Nine? Ten?" Matthew asks.

"Ten."

Another family crisis that I had to deal with.

"Why did we have to go back? I mean I know Grandma was sick, but why did we go? You could have sent her money instead."

I look around. Two more couples in their late twenties come in and stop close to us. One of the women looks at me and then says something to her friends. They all give an uninhibited laugh. A mocking laugh that one would have at a cougar.

"Mom, did you hear what I said?" Matthew asks again, looking at the woman who laughed.

I see him surfing the crowd for people who might know. Then he turns toward me and asks again, "Did you hear?"

"I did, I did. Of course I did. Why are you asking?"

"Because you didn't answer," he says.

I'm surprised he couldn't remember. Keeran and I had a big fight before we left. He didn't want Matthew to come with me. Eventually, he gave up and signed the travel consent.

"We had to go because your grandma got sick, and your grandpa didn't know how to deal with it. They wanted me to go. I had to," I say.

Why is he asking all these questions after so many years? It doesn't matter. What matters is that he's here with me.

Matthew pays the bill, and we're heading back to Harbourfront Centre. The ceremony is to start in one hour. We still have time.

A throbbing headache brings me back to the anxiety of the awards ceremony. I'm happy that Matthew's here with me, but I'm afraid he might feel betrayed when I go on stage.

"Mom, you seem so absent-minded, you look like you're not here. What's going on?" Matthew asks as we stop in the main hallway.

"Nothing, it's nothing, really," I say, moving my purse from one shoulder to the other.

I wish I could tell him how I feel. I wish I could find the courage to tell him he's the reason why I'm here, waiting to receive the award. That my coming to Canada was my blessing and my curse. That, even if I'd been able to go back in time, I wouldn't have changed anything. Instead, I look around as if I expected someone, and then I hear my name.

"Ana Owen? *Félicitations pour gagner le prix,*" says a woman whom I don't recognize. I look at her and don't know what to say. "I'm Claire Martel," she says, kissing me on both cheeks the Quebec way. "We met in Montreal last year, remember?" she says. "*En tout cas, je dois m'en aller. On se revoit après la cérémonie.*"

I know I've met her, but I cannot remember exactly when and where. I need a few seconds to dig into my memory.

"Claire, of course. Hi. Good to see you," I say gripping onto her hand as if she were there to save me from drowning.

"Claire, this is my son Matthew. He lives in Romania. He moved there; can you believe that?" I say.

She smiles at Matthew and shakes his hand.

"Mom, are you still mad at me because of that?" Matthew asks.

His trembling lips make him look like a little boy ready to cry after he's admitted he did something wrong.

"Why do you think I'm mad?" I ask him.

I look at him and for a split second I see myself twenty-five years ago. The restlessness, the despondency, the impulsiveness, the same desperate need for acceptance and approval. At this moment, the crag that has separated our lives starts to crumble, letting the sky in, through small cracks at first and then in full sight. I grab his hand and go to the first floor.

How can I fill up the space between us when words have lost their significance? Meaningless words. Hurtful words. Deceiving words. I open my mouth, but nothing comes out. As a mother, I have a higher duty, a responsibility that supersedes passion, love, sex, chemistry, and relationships. Because, as a parent, I'm expected to suck it up and move on. None of my problems matter. My son expects me to be happy, available, responsible, supportive, encouraging, knowledgeable, and, above all, beautiful. Even if I live one continent away.

I watch Claire as she makes her way to the main auditorium where the ceremony is to take place. She stops to shake hands with the Editor-in-Chief of a top Canadian publisher. I know him from past events, although we've never really connected.

I do remember Claire. I've read all her books. Her memoir, *Place Vendôme*, has been shortlisted for Scotiabank Giller Prize and won Canada Reads in 2014. Her books reminded me of my childhood back in Romania, of my dad, and his fascination with everything French. *Non, je ne regrette rien.*

The crowd is getting bigger. I let Matthew finish his story and go toward a group of people whom I recognize. I wave at former co-workers who also know Keeran, two journalists from the local newspaper, the festival organizing team, and a middle-aged woman from Quebec whose name I can't remember, along with her younger mentee from Halifax. Behind them, the registration table looks like a tornado has swept through name badges, a wooden cash box, a mini-printer, permanent markers, and white labels thrown in disarray.

"Mom, Julia wished she could come," Matthew says looking at me. "You know how much she likes you. She really wanted to be here with you on your big night, but she couldn't. You know that, right? You know that," Matthew repeated, squeezing my arm again.

Do I know that? I'm not sure and I don't care. She's the one who took Matthew away from me, so I don't miss her.

I pull my arm away and head for the washroom. More people are coming in. I quickly look around, hoping to recognize someone, starving for a different kind of conversation, a talk that would shut down the past. How did I turn into this rancorous woman who couldn't forget the day Matthew moved to Romania?

Guiltily, I remember when I first met her, the Thanksgiving dinner when I babbled about Uttwiler Spätlauber apples while my son was lost in her turquoise eyes.

A claustrophobic feeling takes hold of me as we get to the first floor and run into a crowd of people, most of whom I don't know. Cold sweat comes down my spine and my hands almost freeze in half motion before I attach myself to Matthew's elbow like an amoeba extending its pseudopods to swallow up its scavenged prey.

All I can see is smiling faces, hands gesturing in the air, people's backs shaking with laughter, diamond rings sparkling in the diffuse light, a potpourri of human emotions that make the room spin around me.

"Mom, are you okay?" Matthew asks. "You look pale."

The room is getting smaller and smaller. A close-up of enlarged faces and silhouettes. All I can see are splinters of smiles and crooked teeth, hands thrown in the air, curved arms stuck in a group hug, mouths opening and closing uttering words I can no longer hear.

"Mom, are you okay? Are you okay?" I can hear Matthew speak as he grabs my shoulders before I fall into a chair.

When I open my eyes, Matthew is surrounded by a group of people who look unfamiliar.

"What happened? All I can remember is you asking me if I was okay."

"You blacked out, Mom. You must be exhausted. Do you want to go outside and get some fresh air?" he asks.

"No, no, please, I'm fine."

A man in his late fifties, with a navy-blue trench coat casually thrown on his right shoulder, approaches us with a smile.

"Ana Owen?" he says. "It's a pleasure to meet you in person. I'm Malcolm Gardner, the Director of Creative Services at The Living Arts Centre in Mississauga. Let me guess," he says turning toward Matthew, "this is your son who lives in Budapest."

"That's close enough," Matthew says, shaking hands.

After the director of The Living Arts Centre has left, we make our way through the crowd, me scanning the sea of people for familiar faces, Matthew proudly holding me close as if I were a treasure he doesn't want to lose.

"Mom, is Katarina coming? Did you talk to her?" Matthew asks.

"She promised she would come. She arrived this afternoon; her flight got delayed in Copenhagen because of the terrorist attack last night. She was close to the synagogue where one of the shootings took place. Everyone was terrified. They closed the airport," I say as Katarina's voice recounting the event echoes in my head.

We go to the coffee station to grab a Starbucks, half-listening to Matthew. The crowd is getting louder and louder like a bunch of amusement park goers eager to find their wooden horse on a carousel.

"Mom, Julia and I would like you to come and live with us," he says.

"Are you kidding me? No way! Why would I do that? Why do you even ask me? Jesus Christ! What's wrong with you?" I say. "We already talked about this".

Almost everyone turns their heads toward me.

"Mom, relax. I was just asking. You don't need to react like that," Matthew says.

"You're right. I mean, yes, I was just…," I say as someone taps me on the shoulder.

"What? WHAT? What do you want? And who are you, anyway?" I yell as I turn around.

"Ms. Owen? I'm Kevin Dowry. I'm a volunteer with the Harbourfront Centre; I work with the organizing committee. I need to take you backstage in half an hour," he says.

He has a boyish figure in his herringbone jogging trousers and a gingham check shirt. He must be just a few years younger than Matthew.

"Mom, come back with me. You can live with us. Julia would love to have you there. You could give us a hand with Maria, look after her during the day," Matthew says.

I look away. I watch the jogging trousers getting lost in the crowd as I crumple the piece of paper with my speech on it.

"Mom, did you hear what I said?"

I step away from Matthew as an older man with a painter's beret comes toward me, his hand stretched out. The wall behind me doesn't offer me any shelter, I have nowhere to hide. Who is he? What does he want? I turn to leave, but he almost leaps toward me and grabs my hand. In an old-fashioned manner, he lifts it to his lips, kisses it, and leaves. I have no idea who that man is.

"Mom, did you invite Grandpa?" Matthew asks shyly as if he tried not to upset me, not to ask questions that he knows would stir anger and resentment.

"Mom, did you hear what I asked? Is your dad coming?" Matthew insists.

He's not my dad anymore. He's Matthew's grandpa, for what I care, but I don't want to have anything to do with him. To me, he's just a man whose name I have erased from my memory. A vacant nameplate on my childhood door. I don't remember when it was the last time I really felt I had a dad.

"Matthew, I need to go backstage now. Will you keep my seat? I'll come back after that."

He hugs me and strokes my hair in a way that makes me feel like a little girl. A surprising gesture whose significance only the two of us can understand. It was my mom's signature act of affection that soothed my anxiety like peppermint green tea after a heavy meal. Unexpected, refreshing, comforting.

And it became mine when I had to comfort Matthew on the late nights when he couldn't fall asleep.

The Festival Director is waiting for me behind the heavy red curtains, an index card in his left hand, waving at me.

My life has been reduced to a few lines written by a stranger on a piece of paper that he's going to read from, then throw in the garbage, and forget about it. About me.

I walk toward him as if in a trance, looking forward to hearing his voice reading the few words he's scribbled down about me. The regular selling clichés come to mind: immigrant dislocation, acculturation, layered identity, cultural environment, multi-dimensional contexts.

When he starts talking, I almost feel ashamed for having misjudged him.

"Ladies and gentlemen, I have the honour of introducing Ana Owen. Few professions give us as much joy as the one that we're celebrating here tonight. In my twenty-year experience as the Director of this prestigious festival, I've been fortunate to meet quite a few talented individuals whose careers have taken off after winning this award, and I hope this year's winner will continue that tradition. Ladies and gentlemen, congratulations to the winner of the 2015 Debut Fiction Award."

The stage looks bigger and more intimidating than I thought. Squinting in the bright light, I look at the audience trying to tell who's who. I stand there, arms glued to my hips, a few sheets of crumpled paper in my right hand. I smile. I cannot utter any words. I want to thank the Festival Director. Everything seems surreal. I wish Matthew were on stage with me. Where is Katarina? Why didn't she come? What is Dad doing? Is he on another book tour with his partner? Did Mom recognize my voice when she was on life support? Did she hear my confession? Was she mad at my litany of complaints? Disappointed with my lack of resoluteness when it came to relationships? Did Keeran get my email about tonight? Why didn't he respond? Is Maria really sick and that's why Julia couldn't come?

I know I have to speak. I have to thank all these people sitting quietly in the dim lights. No one cares about the emptiness that has almost swallowed up my world. No one cares about the why, they want to hear about the what and how.

My entire focus is on the audience. I finally spot Matthew and wave at him like a little girl dancing in my first ballet show, forgetting the choreography, when to twirl, leap, bend, or glide. Forgetting why I'm here.

* * *

"Every time I go back to Romania, I find a country that I don't recognize. Homeless people holding their babies swaddled in worn-out blankets, unfinished spiral buildings abandoned under the hideous communist urban planning endeavours, an amalgam of rural people who fled to the capital for a better life, ragged panhandlers littering up the downtown taken over by posh expats, les nouveaux riches delivering semiliterate speeches on TV, ego-driven political leaders taking the country to the precipice.

I go back almost like a tourist to a place riddled with memories.

In the country of my memory, people shared a solidarity born out of fear. With their future traced out by a totalitarian state like roads on an ancient map one could hardly read, they learned how to enjoy the small things that filled the void in their lives: reading samizdat novels hand-copied by benevolent smugglers who evaded censorship, watching local theatre performances that featured Maria Callas's bel canto technique, attending art shows by Sabin Bălaşa, whose surrealist paintings and portraits of the Ceauşescu family made him famous.

What I remember is my old neighbourhood, inundated by the fragrance of jasmine and false acacia trees blooming in May, the walks home from school when we played pretend couples passing on a makeshift wedding band to each other.

'Do you know that, if you kiss someone on the lips ten times, you get a ring on your finger?' one of us said.

I remember the lake behind our apartment building where we swam in summertime and then played tag until we were out of breath, the silly games we came up with to tease the younger kids, the admiration we felt for the windsurfers who waved at us as they glided along the shore.

Now the only sight from my parents' balcony is a dumping ground that separates the lake from the hanging flower pots filled with geraniums whose scent is carried indoors on breezy summer days."

I close the book and run my hand over the raised image of Corvins' Castle on the front cover, a Gothic Renaissance fortress that my editor picked as being representative for my story. I wasn't so sure about his choice, but I liked the texture of the embossed letters: oily, smooth, like perfectly roasted coffee beans. I close my eyes and trace each word as if it were written in Braille, made up of dots and dashes that bring the title to life: "*No One Will Remember You.*"

I did it. It's over. After a few minutes of applause that make me bow like an actress at the end of a performance, I go back into the foyer where I get hugged by people I've never met. I do my best to answer their questions, afraid that I might say something wrong. What is the right thing to say, anyway? They want to know how I decided to write the book, if I'll keep writing, and if my book will be translated into other languages.

I look for Matthew. He stands by one of the doors. I see his lips moving and feel grateful for his silent, "I love you, Mom."

Emozione

It's been a few days since I received the award. Matthew has gone back to Romania, and I sit home alone thinking of all the years when I dreaded that this might happen. My son moved to my own country. I wonder what his life is really like in Bucharest. I wonder if Keeran is happy without us. I think of Katarina's prolonged silence when the phone rings. I let it go to voicemail, but whoever called hung up. Half an hour later, she shows up at my door.

When I open it, she steps in and hugs me before I get to say anything.

I breathe in. She smells like white peach and bergamot, with an undertone I cannot recognize until I close my eyes and sink my face into her hair – a woody texture of musk and patchouli. She's wearing my favourite perfume. *Emozione*. Feminine and sensual. Pure emotion.

We stay like that for a long minute, lost for the second time in an embrace that gives me a sensation of weightlessness as if I were an astronaut flying into space.

"So, how was it last night?"

"Well, it would've been perfect if you'd showed up."

"Are you mad at me?" she says moving away just a few inches. We're still holding hands like two dancers drifting apart in a musical interlude.

"How can I be mad? Please come inside. I want to hear all about your trip to India."

"Ana, you know I don't want to talk about it. Please accept that. Can I still come in?" she says letting go of my hands.

I pull her inside and almost follow her into the bathroom as she closes the door behind her with a cheerful laugh that fills up the room.

"Let's make some tea," she yells over the running water.

The fragrance of the jasmine green tea that I've saved for her return adds to the fruity mist she's left behind.

We sit together on the vintage lime green loveseat I've found at a garage sale and sip our tea.

"Why don't you tell me about you? What did I miss? I can't believe Matthew has a baby," Katarina says and then continues after seeing my disappointed face. "Okay, let's make a deal. You can ask only three questions about my trip."

"Deal. Let's see. Hm, was it worth it?"

"Yes, it was."

"That's it? No details? No sub-stories about how enlightened you felt or how you decided to come back and throw out all your belongings, live a minimalist life, not attached to anything and anyone?"

"Well, it did cross my mind, but I'm too attached to my purses, my lipsticks, and a few people," she says as her eyes darken in a squint.

"What was one thing that you missed?"

235

"I lacked quite a few things, but what I missed the most was our walk in Erindale Park. The dinners, the talk, your stories about Romania, I missed you."

Is this the Katarina I knew? Who used to challenge me on almost everything I said, laughing at my anger, telling me not to take myself too seriously? The woman who sits in my living room looks the opposite of a Charlotte Brontë character that I associated her with in the past: a fiery spirit whose refusal to compromise inspired me to move on.

"Okay, the last question. Did you… did you meet anyone while you were there? I mean…" I ask.

"I know what you mean. No, I didn't. That's not why I went to India," she says.

I stroke her hair with both hands, cupping her face in a gesture reminiscent of my first days as a new mother. When I turn my head, I catch a glimpse of a U-Haul truck.

"What's up with the U-Haul truck blocking my driveway?" I ask.

With a smile that makes her teeth look even whiter against a tanned complexion, Katarina pulls her blush cashmere cardigan over her shoulders and leans toward me, "I'm moving in."

THE END

Acknowledgements

This book was possible thanks to my brilliant editor Alexandra Leggat's tremendous support and my publisher Diana Krupensky's unconditional faith in me.

Thank you to all my creative writing instructors at University of Toronto School of Continuing Studies (SCS) for guiding me on my writing journey. I'm grateful to Dr. Ranjini George for believing in my story.

I dedicate this book to all the immigrants who dare to dream and rise strong above life's challenges.

Manufactured by Amazon.ca
Bolton, ON